Praise For

DEVELOPING A DISCIPLE

Only three chapters into *Developing a Disciple: Book 2*, I was convicted and challenged to obey God and grow in my walk with Christ. The lessons have challenged me, as many things do, to slow down and turn off the background noise so I can hear how the Holy Spirit is guiding me. I've already followed up with old friends I have evangelized to see how they are doing and to reengage them in spiritual conversations. This book has also convicted me of my disregard and blocking out of the promptings the Spirit gives me.

I believe this book will significantly affect the Body as a whole. The way Greg has conveyed biblical truths is a beautiful reflection of what we find in Scripture. The lessons combine our reliance upon God and the spiritual side to have real growth and change while not neglecting our responsibility as believers to make war on the flesh and walk continually in obedience. I think this is a much-needed message!

—**Jesse Ward**, momentum coordinator, *The Pursuit Church*

***

Developing a Disciple: Book 2 is a book that not only becomes a joy to read, but also challenges your every understanding of what being a Child of God is. Every one of us has the call on our lives to the Great Commission. The book Mr. Vannatta has put together gives the reader in-depth insight into the true responsibility that is, all the while providing practical and understandable best practices to help us in the journey of sharing the good news to the world around us. All too often, the Holy Spirit's impact on our lives is missed, swept under the rug, or just plain ignored, but not in *Developing a Disciple*. The Holy Spirit takes center stage as one of the main characters in our Christian faith and daily walk.

Developing a Disciple delves into the importance of knowing, building a relationship with, and recognizing and creating a solid understanding of how the Holy Spirit works in and guides our lives. Most importantly, Mr. Vannatta challenges us to not just sit on the sidelines but take an active participant role in sharing the gospel and helping the reader in that challenge by giving sound advice and recommendations on how to reach the lost while still building up our own faith and spiritual health at the same time. This is not a religious book but a guide to help one become a more powerful man of faith.

—**J. Jefferson White**, operations management

***

Book 2 of *Developing a Disciple* takes you down a path as a reader that will help transcend your understanding of the Holy Spirit, the call on your life, the application of your faith, the power of prayer, how all that feeds your soul's ability to serve others—and most important—your service to God. The responsibility to care for the church body is not a responsibility that rests solely on the title of minister or pastor; in developing a disciple, we see that responsibility at the forefront in the life of every believer in Christ.

The author takes the time to walk you through the obstacles and the process of overcoming the challenges you will most certainly face in walking out the responsibilities of being a believer who cares for the church body as well as the lost. This book is not a sit-back-and-read book; it is a call to action for all who have come to know the Lord and understand the responsibility that comes with it. All who read will be both blessed and empowered to serve God in a more applicable and meaningful way. Every believer should have this book of learning and action in their library that can be passed down to others as they mature in their spiritual walk.

—Joshua Burlison

***

Developing a Disciple lays out in 12 lessons how to grow into an authentic, fruitful disciple of Jesus Christ. Each of the 12 lessons works to build on the critical components of becoming a disciple. All can and should be practically applied to the daily walk of a disciple or anyone striving to become a disciple of Jesus Christ.

One of my favorite things about this discipleship tool is the questions at the end of each lesson. They challenged me to self-reflect on my current status and spurred me to apply what I learned in each lesson to my daily life. Also, these questions will lead to great discussion amongst the group members. If the church community at large were to take part in this discipleship training, and truly surrender to the Lordship of Jesus Christ upon their lives, the church community would be radically transformed, and thus, the secular community all around it would also be fundamentally impacted for Jesus.

One thing that I find very refreshing is that this discipleship tool focuses on spiritual and physical transformation. I am excited about how the Lord will use this discipleship tool to transform many lives for their benefit and HIS purpose!
—Trent Vandervorst

***

What does it take to become a disciple? This is a great question that I believe has plagued churches for years. We talk a good game about how people need to be disciples and have discipleship classes, but more times than not, churches don't follow through. And this tends to leave many "churched" people missing an essential part of their faith journey. Greg does a fantastic job at bringing discipleship to the people of the churches While he does it in such a way that it is easy to understand, causes you to dig deep into the questions Greg poses at the end of each chapter.

I would have to say that one of my favorite parts of this book comes from the first two chapters, where Greg talks about the Holy Spirit. Growing up in a Presbyterian church, I do not remember them ever talking about the Holy Spirit at all, and then I went to an Assembly of God church in college, which was tough to adjust to. It was like one extreme to the next. Neither church seemed to talk in-depth about the Holy Spirit, which is why I loved how simple yet deep Greg made these chapters on this subject. I feel like this book will bless a lot of people. Thanks, Greg, for writing it.
—**Jesse Barlow**, lead pastor, *The Pursuit, Stanley, ND*

***

This teaching can absolutely encourage believers to actively seek the Holy Spirit's wisdom and guidance, which can profoundly enhance their spiritual journey and relationship with Jesus. Greg Vanatta paints a very clear picture of the Holy Spirit's multifaceted role. He explains the significance of the Holy Spirit in the process of justification, sanctification, and glorification, advocating for its crucial role in daily Christian living.

Given the understanding of the Holy Spirit's role in our lives, enables us to apply our gifts better to expand God's Kingdom. The Holy Spirit's indwelling, baptism, and filling are distinct experiences, with the baptism occurring once and the filling occurring multiple times. We can encourage believers to seek wisdom and guidance from the Holy Spirit, emphasizing the need for humility, patience, and consistent engagement with scripture. I believe the modern church could be more effective in building disciples. Teachings like Greg's can, without a doubt, aid in that process.

—**Geoff Bagi**, worship director/pastor

DEVELOPING A DISCIPLE

BOOK 2

GREG VANNATTA

Published by KHARIS PUBLISHING, an imprint of KHARIS MEDIA LLC.
Copyright © 2025 Greg Vannatta
ISBN-13: 978-1-63746-275-1
ISBN-10: 1-63746-275-1
Library of Congress Control Number: 2025930401
All rights reserved. This book or parts thereof may not be reproduced in any form, stored in a retrieval system, or transmitted in any form by any means - electronic, mechanical, photocopy, recording, or otherwise - without prior written permission of the publisher, except as provided by United States of America copyright law.
Unless otherwise noted, all Scripture is taken from the NASB: NEW AMERICAN STANDARD BIBLE®, copyright© Holy2021 by The Lockman Foundation. Used by permission.
ESV: Scriptures marked ESV are taken from THE HOLY BIBLE, ENGLISH STANDARD VERSION (ESV): Scriptures taken from THE HOLY BIBLE, ENGLISH VERSION® Copyright© 2001, 2024 by Crossway, a publishing ministry of Good News Publishers. Used by permission.
CSB: The Christian Standard Bible. Copyright © 2017, 2022 by Holman Bible Publishers. Used by permission. Christian Standard Bible®, and CSB® are federally registered trademarks of Holman Bible Publishers, all rights reserved.
NIV: Scripture taken from THE HOLY BIBLE, NEW INTERNATIONAL VERSION®. Copyright© 1973, 1978, 1984, 2011, 2o24 by Biblica, Inc.™. Used by permission of Zondervan.
All KHARIS PUBLISHING products are available at special quantity discounts for bulk purchase for sales promotions, premiums, fund-raising, and educational needs. For details, contact:
Kharis Media LLC
Tel: 1-630-909-3405
support@kharispublishing.com
www.kharispublishing.com

CONTENTS

Preface 11

Introduction... 17

1. Knowing the Holy Spirit 29

2. How Does the Holy Spirit Guide us in our Witness? 43

3. Answering the Call from the Lord 56

4. Applying the Word to our Actions 68

5. Knowing What Soil we are Working With 80

6. Knowing our Strength in Jesus 92

7. Praying for Others and Quiet Times 104

8. Reading the Bible to Understand 117

9. Building Patience... 129

10. Having the Mind of Christ 141

11. Caring for the Church Body........................ 152

12. Fundamentals of Evangelism 164

PREFACE

Now that we have completed Book 1 Developing a Disciple, we need to dive into the conditioning of a disciple and what this means. Conditioning ourselves plays a big role in what we do as disciple-makers and how we approach living a life honorable to the Lord. Conditioning helps us lay down our selfish or self-centered motives, allowing us to hear the Holy Spirit when He speaks to us; it builds our faith and lays a solid foundation of why we believe in the breathed and inspired Word of God. Conditioning ourselves is never fun. It takes self-discipline, patience, understanding, wisdom, repentance, and forgiveness.

We allow God to search the deepest areas of our hearts to reveal the hidden things we need to rid ourselves of in order to have the fullness of Christ purify our hearts and minds. This also allows us to have the perspective that we will never see the fullness of Christ until we realize that everything else is empty.

This conditioning never ends but is just like our testimonies, it's a lifelong requirement that allows us to walk in the Will of God and complete the tasks that He has set before us.

One of the most important parts of the conditioning of a believer is how we are applying the Word of God to our daily lives and how we are letting the Word of God renew our minds every single day. Next, how are we sharing the good news, and how are we reaching lost souls to build the Church of Christ to glorify the name of Jesus? We must have an understanding of some basic fundamentals in conditioning before we start applying everything we have learned. Most believers today just go out and try to evangelize, not being aware of the damage that can occur if one evangelizes with selfish or prideful motivation.

Many times before, I have seen arrogance come out in a believer, and it turns away the non-believer. There was no plausibility structure to give real living evidence that could persuade or convince the non-believer to believe in the Word of God. The only thing this can result in is psychological damage that not only leaves the non-believer confused and still searching, but also leaves the believer with a faith that no longer has power and strength. You can see why the conditioning aspect is so valuable for us to work on, invest in, and continue to develop daily.

As we work through this book, the questions in the lessons will begin to grow spiritually deeper, more challenging, require more thought, place us in a

DEVELOPING A DISCIPLE

position of being uncomfortable, and bring us closer to our Heavenly Father. We will begin with knowing who the Holy Spirit is and how He works in our lives, ending with the fundamentals of evangelism.

You will meet weekly with your group, so here are some guidelines to help structure your gatherings. Remember, each lesson should take two weeks—up to three in some cases. At first, it may seem slow to spend two weeks on one lesson, but the point is to learn how to dig deeper and start applying good hermeneutics or study habits. This will be challenging; everyone has a personal life with many responsibilities to their families, churches, work, friends, etc. I want everyone to know it is ok if there is a time when your group needs to take a break. Rest is critical and very important. If we are not well-rested, it is next to impossible to stay focused on what is most important in our relationship with Jesus.

- **Quiet Time** – This is a time of personal devotion between you and the Lord. The term is to remind you to quiet your heart and mind during your personal devotional time. There are specific Scriptural passages in the Quiet Time section of each lesson. Read these passages and meditate on them, asking the Holy Spirit to reveal or illuminate in your heart the truth of God's Word in the passage. This takes some time to gain consistency, but as you do this daily, you will find consistency and a deeper love for God's Word.

- **Each weekly gathering** with your group should consist of an opening time of prayer for one another, and then taking some time to catch up with how the week has been. It is good to get in the habit of asking how you can help support and pray for one another during the week.

- **Conditioning of a Disciple** – This is meant to be a life-long process that continues to challenge us daily in our walk with the Lord. Conditioning requires us as believers to go through some difficult times and times of rejoicing or celebrating. As a believer, you have to keep your heart and mind focused on Christ and not is what's going on around the world, but be prepared for anything that could happen. The Lord—and living in His light and truth—is our priority as believers. Building good habits and consistency is key to our growth and development as believers living in the community and culture of the kingdom of God here on earth (the church).

- **The weekly exercise plan** – This is to help develop a routine of consistency which promotes the growth and development of having personal discipline. This shouldn't replace your time in Scripture; it should be a supplement to help build a character of discipline. Spiritual and physical strength are not the same, but they do go hand-in-hand as we continue to grow and develop in our relationship with Jesus. The reps help to have consistency in the approach to each lift, which also helps build muscle just like you will be building a spiritual muscle through the study time. The key is to use light weights, work through the reps, stay focused, and be honest with yourself that it is ok if not all the workout gets done. One goal of the weekly exercise plan is not only to develop discipline, but also to realize that no matter how physically strong we get, we still cannot live this life on earth in our own strength. We need the strength of Christ in our lives. A second goal is to demonstrate the challenge of building healthy habits and discipline to keep you focused for various lengths of time. The weekly exercise plan shows the reality of how building strength can exhaust us and cause pain and suffering through being sore from the exercise routine. But when we work in the strength of Christ, we can endure the hardships, challenges, and trials of life because we don't operate in our own strength.

The goal of this book is to get you to know, believe, and have strength in the Holy Spirit so that you can go out and share the good news of Jesus Christ with Love. If we don't share out of Love, then we have nothing.

As you go through this book, it is important to continue to pray for your brothers, encourage them, build them up, and walk alongside them. Have an understanding that we are all at different levels of our walk, so patience will be essential. Be patient with yourselves and others, as this is a journey and pilgrimage to develop a deep love for Jesus Christ. Take your time going through the lessons. Be sure to take the spiritual audit before and after you have gone through all the lessons. This is the same spiritual audit as in the first book, Developing a Disciple (DAD) (Covenant Press, 2024).

INTRODUCTION

YOUR SPIRITUAL AUDIT FOR GROWING AND DEVELOPING INTO THE MAN GOD WANTS YOU TO BE

Why conduct a spiritual audit on yourself? Does a spiritual audit seem to be a waste of valuable time and resources? Absolutely not! Taking the time to conduct a spiritual audit over your life is a skilled discipline to help gauge where you currently are spiritually in your Christian walk. This spiritual audit requires no copies of receipts, bank statements, or pending payments for debts. Why? Because the full price for the redemption of your sins has already been paid by Jesus Christ with His finished work on the Cross. Knowing that the payment for your sins has already been covered by the shed blood of Jesus Christ is enough to make this spiritual audit a primary focus to ensure your focus has been and is still on Jesus Christ and the kingdom of God.

As you progress through this spiritual audit, I encourage you to take time to reflect on your personal life, reflect on involvement with your church, reflect on your commitment to family and friends, and most important, meditate on God's Word and pray. This spiritual audit will not work out well if you are not spending time in Scripture meditating and praying over what God is speaking to you through His Word. Take your time and be as specific as you can in this spiritual audit, working with one another in displaying the fruit of the Spirit (Galatians 5: 22 – 23). Please use a notebook to write down your observations, revelations, challenges, and changes that you need to make to become a godlier man in pursuit of God's heart. Discuss with your group.

1. **Am I content with who I currently am and who God is transforming me to become?**
    - What areas of my life am I the most familiar with? What are the elements of these areas? (i.e., sports, movies, tv, camping).
    - Do these areas of my life affect my identity and character?
    - Are there areas of my life that I give more attention to than my personal family, and spiritual family?

- What is causing me to place my attention on the outward influences of the world over being influenced by Scripture?
- What changes or disciplines do I need to place my focus back on Scripture and Jesus Christ?

2. **Am I developing spiritually and becoming less religious?** Remember that the Pharisees were religious, but Jesus Christ was spiritual. The differences between religion and spirituality are a matter of gaining and keeping control. As male leaders, we tend to draw near the path of gaining control over our situations. As we look at Jesus Christ, we see that Jesus was always in pursuit of only the will of the Father and never pursuing His own control.

- What characteristics do I have that make me want to remain or gain control?
- Has gaining control caused stress, doubt, fear, anxiety, or uncertainty in my life?
- What control can I give up and still be in the freedom of Jesus? Is this necessary?
- Is there a deeper source to my need for control? What is this deeper origin that I need to uproot?
- How will I give up control over things that I cannot and do not need to control? What

will this do to my character and virtue? (Colossians 3: 1 – 25).

3. **Is there evidence from my personal family, spiritual family, and friends of the authenticity of my spirituality?**

- If an individual from my family, church, friend, or employer was interviewed about my character. Would they provide a true testimony to evidence of spiritual growth in my life through the study and application of Scripture?
- What evidence would my personal family state about my spiritual growth?
- Do I have a love for the lost with a mission mentality to preach the gospel to all nations? (Mark 16: 15).
- Is my love for the church clear among the church body in the way I serve the body of Christ?
- What changes do I need to make to become more disciplined in the display of my spiritual walk, having a true testimony of the transformation of becoming a new creature in Christ Jesus?

4. **What are my follow-through and follow-up principles in my daily walk?**

- What resources do I currently use to help in my follow-up and follow-through in my daily responsibilities personally, professionally, and spiritually?
- What causes me to not follow-up or follow-through in my responsibilities personally, professionally, and spiritually?
- Has my follow-up or follow-through affected another individuals either negatively or positively? What happened with the other individual's perspective towards your character, integrity, and testimony of being a believer in Jesus Christ?
- What areas of my follow-up and follow-through need to improve to display the character and virtue of Jesus in my daily walk as a Christian?
- Do I need to repent and ask for forgiveness from a brother in Christ Jesus due to a lack of follow-through, follow-up, or avoidance of a phone call, text message, or other form of communication?

5. **Am I having quiet times in Scripture deepening and developing my spiritual walk?**

- Do I have an area dedicated to have my quiet time for the study of Scripture,

meditation of Scripture, and intentional time spent in prayer?
- What distractions bring challenges to my quiet times, both inside and outside the house?
- Am I spending time daily communicating with God in prayer? If not, what is distracting you from communicating with God regularly throughout the day, and what needs to change to make sure this communication continues?
- Are my quiet times bringing me closer to God, or do I still have some uncertainties about my faith?
- What must I do to help find the evidence needed for any uncertainty I have in the truth of Scripture?

6. Has my prayer life improved, or is it improving?

- Am I continuously looking to spend time in prayer each day?
- Am I praying more for the needs of others rather than my own needs?
- Am I praying for the Lord's will and not my own self-intentions?
- Has prayer brought discipling in my daily Christian walk?

- Has prayer been something that I have fallen in love with and want to be part of everyday as a Christian?

7. **Is there a ministry to which I am feeling called to serve in the church?**
   - Has the Lord laid upon my heart a specific ministry in which to serve faithfully within the church?
   - Do I have a fear in serving in a church ministry? Are these manufactured fears (fear, anxiety, time, dedication, loyalty)? How does the "fear of the Lord" reflect my want to serve in a specific ministry in the church?
   - Will serving in a specific church ministry help my spiritual walk, growth, and development in understanding Scripture?
   - Why is serving in a specific church ministry important to my own walk and helping others grow through discipling?
   - Am I able to disciple in a specific church ministry?

8. **Do I have a "fear of the Lord"?** In Hebrew, the word is yirah, meaning an awe of the Lord and His majesty along with the trembling of His wrath.

- Is the "fear of the Lord" relevant to the modern church? What does this mean for us today?
- Am I in a constant state of "awe" of how big and great God truly is? If not, why am I not in a state of "awe"? Do I still have uncertainties about my faith, Scripture, who Jesus truly is, the application of Scripture in the modern world?
- Are all hardships in life part of God's wrath, or do the hardships of life bring us closer to God?
- Can the hardships of life be a gift we are able to value and appreciate, to give God glory?
- What must I do to have a "fear of the Lord" that causes my heart to be in "awe" of who God is bringing me closer to God?

9. Am I displaying a genuine humility and humbleness in my daily walk?

- What does it mean to display genuine and organic humility and humbleness as a Christian in a modern world?
- How have I displayed humility in the past week? Month? Year?
- Is my humbleness true, or does it reflect a self-defeating attitude taking away the value

of myself being made in the image and likeness of God? (Genesis 1: 26 -28).
- Do time commitments reflect the humility and humbleness of my character, integrity, and virtue? Do I have issues keeping time commitments?
- Why are humility and a humble heart important to my Christian walk?

10. Am I being fed spiritually at home and not just on a Sunday morning?

- What am I doing at home and during my spare time to continue to feed myself spiritually through Scripture?
- What is keeping me from feeding myself spiritually at home in my personal time?
- Am I able to feed my family spiritually at home? Or do we rely only on the Sunday morning sermon to be fed as a family? What difference does this make?
- What are my obligations and responsibilities at home to make sure that my family and I are fed spiritually and not stagnant in our Spiritual walk?
- If necessary, what will I do to make a change to start feeding my family and myself spiritually at home? What will the results of this be for my family and myself?

11. Am I continuing to be obedient in the small obligations and responsibilities placed upon me as a follower of Jesus Christ?

- Have I been obedient in the calling that God has placed upon my heart, walking with a humble heart in humility to work in the will of God?

- What commitments have I backed out on in the past 3 months? What were the results of this in my spiritual walk? Did I come closer to the Lord or not? Did it help someone else come closer to the Lord?

- What do I need to do to make sure my time is always given to God to glorify His name and build His kingdom? What will I do when the responsibilities of life get to be too much, leaving little time to gather with the saints and build God's kingdom?

- Am I too busy to commit myself to working within the plan and will of God? What effects has this had on spending time in Scripture? Is this beneficial or not?

- What changes do I need to make today to walk in the commitment I have for the Lord? Jesus gave everything for me, my family, the church, and all people on earth. What is my struggle in giving back to speak of the glory of the Lord?

12. Do I have joy that comes from the Lord, or am I still clinging to the manufactured joys of the world?

- Do I understand the true Joy of the Lord? What is this, Joy?

- Are there things in life that bring me more joy than reading Scripture, spending time in prayer, gathering with the saints, or serving in a specific ministry that would help another individual grow and develop spiritually?

- Why do I choose to receive joy from the world rather than Jesus? What must I repent of and change to have a heart transformation that draws me closer to God? (Ezekiel 11: 14-21).

- Is repentance and forgiveness a part of my daily Christian walk? Does this bring joy into my heart knowing that Jesus is the only one that can remove all sin now and forever?

- What is my biggest challenge in rejoicing daily about who Jesus is, what He did for all humankind, and knowing that He will soon return one day, holding true to His promise? (Revelation 1: 7). (Vannatta,G., Developing a Disciple Book 1, Spiritual Audit, Covenant Press, 2024)

1

KNOWING THE HOLY SPIRIT

I can't think of one thing that is more missed in today's modern church than the teaching of the Holy Spirit. It almost seems taboo for modern churches to teach about the Holy Spirit; I believe that is due to ignorance on the subject. I think it is safe to say that many believers have an understanding of the indwelling of the Holy Spirit at the point of conversion, and asking Jesus into our hearts that we may have salvation. However, it goes a lot deeper than just the indwelling of the Holy Spirit of the human heart. We can start at **Genesis 1:1-2**: "In the beginning God created the heavens and the earth. The earth was formless and void, and darkness was over the surface of the deep, and the Spirit of God was moving over the surface of the waters."

The Holy Spirit was evident at the beginning of creation, knowing that we need the Holy Spirit to sustain life on earth fulfilling the mission of God. He uses His Holy Spirit in many different ways throughout Scripture with spiritual gifts, baptism of the Holy Spirit, the filling of the Holy Spirit, guidance, protection, and communication to all believers. These are just a few examples of how God uses the Holy Spirit in our lives every single day. It was relative at the time of creation and is relative today. The beautiful thing about the Holy Spirit is that you see He never changes and always works in the same way, under the authority of Jesus.

When someone first becomes a believer, there are multiple processes that happen to that person: Justification, sanctification, salvation, and glorification, but the one thing that I have seen a lot of confusion about is the indwelling of the Holy Spirit. In **Ephesians 1:13-14,** we learn, "In Him, you also, after listening to the message of truth, the gospel of your salvation – having also believed, you were sealed in Him with the Holy Spirit of promise, who is given as a pledge of our inheritance, with a view to the redemption of God's *own* possession, to the praise of His glory."

We received an inheritance to help guide us every day to walk in the Will of God, we were all baptized into one body. **1 Corinthians 12:13** says, "…for by one Spirit are we all baptized into one body, whether Jews or Greeks, whether slave or free; and we were all made to drink into one spirit."

We see how we have been given a helper to guide us through every situation, every trial, and every tribulation that we will come up against. We also receive teaching and help in our weaknesses.

Knowing just a little about the Holy Spirit now, why wouldn't we want to teach on this? If we avoid teaching this, it only leads us to a quenching and grieving of the Holy Spirit. Quenching, in this case, means to extinguish rather than to satisfy. The result is that we can, at times, work in our own strength and lean into our own understanding rather than leaning into the help of the Holy Spirit for guidance and direction. The only reason I can think that it would be the case for not teaching on the Holy Spirit is this: When you allow the Holy Spirit to work in the way God wants, He takes away our control, our structure, our projected plans, our titles or the degrees we hold, and our accomplishments, leading to a complete and total submission and surrender to Jesus Christ.

Now, I can't think of a more humbling place to be than having the presence of the Holy Spirit lead us. It causes us to have humility, be vulnerable, and be open to God's timing. I understand how this can seem scary to most believers, as not always being in charge does have a very real-world experience of chaos in one's life.

But if we do everything according to our ways, how then can we receive wisdom, a helper, guidance, spiritual gifts, conviction, and love? **Isaiah 11:2** tells us, "And the spirit of the Lord shall rest upon him, the spirit of wisdom and understanding, the spirit of counsel and strength, the spirit of knowledge and the fear of the Lord."

We should all seek wisdom and understanding which leads to the fear of the Lord. The Holy Spirit alone can give us an understanding of Scripture, and this is when Scripture becomes illuminated in the human heart by the Holy Spirit, to transform the heart into something beautiful.

The Holy Spirit is God's Spirit being part of the Trinity to help continue God's mission on earth here and now. The Holy Spirit was given to us as a helper that would expand God's kingdom on earth, helping to build a culture and community of God's kingdom. The Holy Spirit displays the character, reputation, and virtue of Jesus Christ. With the Holy Spirit having the personality and character of a gentleman, He waits for us to ask Him or call upon Him as our helper given to us from Jesus Christ. The Holy Spirit is who gives us our strength while Jesus Christ is currently seated on the throne of heaven. The Holy Spirit is our helper.

Now that we have laid a foundation of who the Holy Spirit is, let's look at the indwelling, baptism, and filling of the Holy Spirit. As I stated earlier, there is much confusion between these three subjects. There are different terms used to describe the various activities, and because of this, it really isn't surprising that there is some confusion with regard to the relationship of these things to one another. First, the indwelling of the Holy Spirit happens at the time of conversion. This is part of the gift of salvation, the down payment of our inheritance.

Second is the baptism of the Holy Spirit. This can only be given by Jesus at the appointed time He wants to give this. Third is the filling of the Holy Spirit; again, this is only given by Jesus at the appointed time He wants to give it. Baptism and filling are two separate things from the indwelling of the Holy Spirit. The baptism of the Holy Spirit is a one-time occurrence for the believer and never repeats. The filling of the Holy Spirit can occur multiple times in a believer's life. Think of it as every time we pray for strength and guidance.

1 Corinthians 12:13 states, "For by one spirit are we all baptized into one body, whether we Jews or Greeks, whether slaves or free; and we were all made to drink into one spirit." Then we see in both Ephesians and Acts that the filling happens multiple times. **Ephesians 5:18** states, "…and do not get drunk with wine, for that is dissipation, but be filled with the Spirit." **Acts 2:4** says, "Then they were all filled with the Holy Spirit and began to speak in different tongues, as the Spirit enabled them" (CSB).

Knowing that there are three aspects of how the Holy Spirit works in the believer's life can be one of the most encouraging assurances when dealing with the struggles and hardships of life. We have hope knowing that the Holy Spirit is omnipresent and always by us to help, to give us guidance and direction. The Holy Spirit has been given to us as a gift and should always be cherished and treasured. It is impossible for any believer to make it through life without the help of the Holy Spirit. In fact, the Holy Spirit is the oil in our lamp that guides the way down the path God wants us to walk.

I can recall times in my personal walk as a new believer when I didn't have a good understanding of the Holy Spirit. I had a lot of confusion and a lot of questions in regard to the workings of the Holy Spirit. The one thing I wanted so badly was the baptism of the Holy Spirit. At that time in my walk, little did I know that this is only a gift Jesus gives when He is ready to give it to us at the time of conversion. It took a few years for me to understand this because I was still dealing with past guilt and honestly doing things that grieved the Holy Spirit.

When I look back now, Jesus was actually teaching me that if I wanted a gift that is so precious, so loving, a sacred gift, then I needed to clean up my act and really live out my dedication to Jesus Christ and continue to help build the kingdom of God. That was a pretty intense statement to hear coming from the Holy Spirit. I thought I was doing pretty good until then! Jesus really has a way of humbling us to purify and purge all impurities of the human heart.

The more I searched and sought the Holy Spirit, the more God revealed to me how the motivation and intentions of a man play a factor in when this gift is given. Some people seek the baptism of the Holy Spirit or the filling of the Holy Spirit because there is power that comes with these. The motivation of some people may be good, while the intention of other individuals might have a selfish or self-centered motivation.

I have seen many times where believers twist, distort, and manipulate believers to the point where their persuasion and influence are so great that the believer is no longer in the Word of God daily, and they are only relying on the emotions and feelings of being a human. Believers are left empty of hope and love because they haven't received this gift. The reality is that this gift can come at any time during a believer's walk, from the time of sanctification to the deathbed, because sanctification is a life-long process. There are no shortcuts in this process; it takes time. This process is relational with the Holy Spirit.

We need to be patient and trust Jesus with this, as He has the perfect timing. This gift is for the act of witnessing just like we see the Apostles and disciples do, so we need to treat this gift as holy and sacred. For us to understand and have wisdom on this subject, we do need to be in the Word constantly without hesitation ask for guidance from the Holy Spirit to have understanding about Him. I pray that you will be filled with the Holy Spirit and let Him guide and lead you in all knowledge and wisdom given by our Lord Christ in the breathed and inspired Word He has given to us.

LESSON 1

Begin your lesson by praying with your group, asking the presence of the Holy Spirit to be with you and guide you.

Memory Verse:

Try your best to memorize the Bible verse. It is ok to struggle with this, as memorization can be difficult. Be sure to extend grace towards one another in memorizing Bible verses. This is to help create consistency and develop a good habit of thinking about Scripture throughout the day.

> ***Ephesians 5:18:*** *"And do not get drunk with wine, for that is dissipation, but be filled with the Spirit."*

Quiet Times:

Personal time of devotion and dedication, spending time in the Scriptures with the Lord.
1 Corinthians 12:7-13 (Monday – Wednesday)
Ephesians 5:15-33 (Thursday – Saturday)
Acts 2: 1-14 (Monday – Wednesday)
Acts 4:29-31 (Thursday – Saturday)

During your quiet times, follow these guidelines and write them in a journal or notebook so that you can share them with your group. Share at least one quiet time with your group. Before sharing a quiet time, please begin by having one of your brothers pray over the group.

Quiet Time – Guideline:

- Be specific in your answers, writing a paragraph for each answer.
- Key point or theme of the passage/verse - What is the author's intent to the original audience?
- Key Words - Repeated words in the text
- Emphasize word(s) - Use a concordance or Bible dictionary to find what the word's context means in your key verse.
- What is the original intent of the author to the original audience?
- Is there a biblical principle from the original audience we can apply in our modern time?
- How will the application of the biblical principle make a difference in your daily walk with the Lord?
- Rewrite your key verse to make it personal to our modern time, without reading yourself into the text.

- How will this verse help you approach a lost person and tell them of the love of Jesus?
- What are the differences and similarities between the original audience and our modern audience?

Lesson 1 Discussion Questions:

Be prepared to discuss the questions from Lesson 1 with your group.

1. What does the indwelling of the Holy Spirit have to do with salvation and how does this reflect your relationship with Jesus?
2. There can be multiple ways that we grieve the Holy Spirit: Lewd expressions, letting your imagination dwell on an impure act, a heart that is covetous, and setting your heart on anything evil are a few examples in a believer's personal walk. Has there been a time when you grieved the Holy Spirit and it has hindered your witness to a non-believer? How and why did the grieving of the Holy Spirit happen? What actions did you take to reconcile and get back on track with your walk?
3. Have you been a part of the grieving of the Holy Spirit in the church body? What effect did this have on your personal walk with the Lord

and keeping you from fully and truly being in His Word daily?
4. How will you help lead the church body away from grieving the Holy Spirit?
5. Why is the Holy Spirit important to you? What happens when you are led by the Holy Spirit in the Word of God daily?
6. What effects does the Holy Spirit have on your personal family, and spiritual family? Why does this matter?
7. How will you allow the Holy Spirit to guide and direct you? What difference will this make in your witness both inside and outside the church?
8. Is there anything holding you back from allowing the Holy Spirit to work in your life today so that you can be a witness to the Kingdom of God and the good news of Jesus?
9. What will your application and follow up action plan be to help your brothers?

The subject of the Holy Spirit is hard to understand as there are so many different points of view on this. However, we need to keep it simple and know that this is a gift from God to be the witness He has called us to be, to build His church, represent His kingdom, and not only love one another, but also love our neighbors as ourselves.

Exercise Plan – Week 1 and Week 2

Monday - chest
- Bench Press (4-5 sets, 15, 12, 10, 8 reps)
- Incline bench press (4-5 sets, 15, 12, 10, 8 reps)
- Dumbbell press (4-5 sets, 15, 12, 10, 8 reps)
- Dumbbell flyes (4-5 sets, 15, 12, 10, 8 reps)
- Chest press (4-5 sets, 15, 12, 10, 8 reps)
- Dips (4-5 sets, 15, 12, 10, 8 reps)
- 20 minutes cardio – seated row, jog, run, elliptical, bike riding

Tuesday – back and abs
- Deadlift (4-5 sets, 15, 12, 10, 8 reps)
- Lat pulldown (4-5 sets, 15, 12, 10, 8 reps)
- Dumbbell rows (4-5 sets, 15, 12, 10, 8 reps)
- Leg raises (4-5 sets, 15, 12, 10, 8 reps)
- Sit-ups (4-5 sets, 15, 12, 10, 8 reps)
- 20 minutes cardio – seated row, jog, run, elliptical, bike riding

Wednesday – shoulders and traps
- Front to back military press (4-5 sets, 15, 12, 10, 8 reps)
- Front raises (4-5 sets, 15, 12, 10, 8 reps)

- Lateral raises (4-5 sets, 15, 12, 10, 8 reps)
- Shrugs (4-5 sets, 15, 12, 10, 8 reps)
- Rear delt raises (4-5 sets, 15, 12, 10, 8 reps)
- 20 minutes cardio – seated row, jog, run, elliptical, bike riding

Thursday – arms

- Bicep curls (4-5 sets, 15, 12, 10, 8 reps)
- Barbell curls (4-5 sets, 15, 12, 10, 8 reps)
- Preacher curls (4-5 sets, 15, 12, 10, 8 reps)
- Hammer curls (4-5 sets, 15, 12, 10, 8 reps)
- Triceps pushdown (4-5 sets, 15, 12, 10, 8 reps)
- Triceps dips (4-5 sets, 15, 12, 10, 8 reps)
- Skull crusher (4-5 sets, 15, 12, 10, 8 reps)
- Triceps extension (4-5 sets, 15, 12, 10, 8 reps)
- 20 minutes cardio – seated row, jog, run, elliptical, bike riding

Friday – legs

- Squats (4-5 sets, 15, 12, 10, 8 reps)
- Leg press (4-5 sets, 15, 12, 10, 8 reps)
- Leg extension (4-5 sets, 15, 12, 10, 8 reps)
- Leg curls (4-5 sets, 15, 12, 10, 8 reps)
- Stiff-leg deadlift (4-5 sets, 15, 12, 10, 8 reps)
- Sitting calf raises (4-5 sets, 15, 12, 10, 8reps)
- Standing calf raises (4-5 sets, 15, 12, 10, 8 reps)

- 20 minutes cardio – seated row, jog, run, elliptical, bike riding

Saturday and Sunday – Recovery

The exercise routine is to help you see measurable results as you go through the study each week. As you rest and recover, be sure your family is always a priority. Your family also comes before the regular exercise routine during the week. It is far more important and valuable that you are spiritually leading your family rather than spending countless hours at the gym or exercising in your home gym. Be intentional with your family and help develop, build, and grow them spiritually, getting to Jesus in a deeper way.

2

HOW DOES THE HOLY SPIRIT GUIDE US IN OUR WITNESS?

Knowing when the Holy Spirit is nudging or calling us to do something requires self-discipline and a need to quiet the mind from the distraction of noises. It's so easy today to be so distracted with all the conveniences of life, that we are unable to hear that small, still voice. With the distractions of work, entertainment, friends, family, vacations, church activities, and so much more, it can be quite difficult to quiet our minds to hear the voice of the Holy Spirit. To hear the Holy Spirit speaking to you takes self-discipline, a sound mind, and both the want and the need to hear from Him. You must take time to be still and quiet.

In my career as a traveling salesman for multiple brands, I know the effects of being too busy to stop and listen for the Holy Spirit. I am always bombarded with phone calls, emails, meetings, customer visits, being on the road, and it seems to never end. Maybe like me, you are always having to find out answers and have an immediate solution for the clientele, which takes a lot of time with a lot of multi-tasking. There is always a situation where focus is needed at a moment's notice. With so many different situations going on throughout the day, you can easily see how frustration, anxiety, and even fear can slowly creep in to distract you. We need to learn to manage our time and activities, and have self-control so we can hear from the Holy Spirit.

With this we also need to see that we love God over the pleasures of the world; it is those pleasures that form the basis for most distractions that keep us so busy that we miss out on hearing the Holy Spirit speak to us. We must come to the realization that worldly pleasures place our hearts at risk of falling back into old ways of living, placing other things before God.

We can look directly at the cross to see this example. **Matthew 27:35** says, "And when they had crucified Him, they divided up His garments among themselves by casting lots."

It's easy to see here that at our Lord's expense of pain, people were still able to put worldly pleasure over their love for the Lord, hindering their ability to hear the Holy Spirit speak to them. **Mark 15:24** tells us this again, "And they crucified Him, and divided up His garments among themselves, casting lots for them to decide what each man should take."

There is always a cost when it comes to the transformation of the human heart, our character, and the process of sanctification. This cost leads to pain and suffering, which is to pick up our cross daily.

If only the soldiers had not chosen to put themselves and pleasure above all else, just maybe they would have heard the Holy Spirit speak to their hearts. Maybe they would have heard the Holy Spirit tell them they were taking the life of the One who loved them so much that He died for them.

How we must reflect on our own lives to make sure that our business is not allowing us to put artificial pleasure before the Lord and the guidance of his Holy Spirit. The act of self-discipline and having patience are truly needed. Today—much like the ancient times—anything can become an altar of idolatry. How many Christians worship their church and take pleasure in this before honoring and worshiping the Lord?

I had the unique experience of this revelation in my own yard, right in front of my house. I sat on the couch, reading a book, and looked out the front window. I noticed that a girl had walked into our front yard, half-dressed and wearing a flamingo blanket to cover herself. Now, this not being a normal activity on our street, I wanted to use caution, not knowing who may be following her.

As I waited a few moments watching this girl, she sat down in our front yard and began to rock back and forth. This really had me concerned at this moment, because I knew something wasn't right. The more I wanted to wait, the more the Holy Spirit kept tugging at my heart to go talk to her. I spoke with my wife and decided I needed to go speak with the girl and see if she was ok. My wife gathered a cup of water and a hooded sweatshirt that we gave the girl to wear so she didn't feel so exposed to the elements.

As I sat down on the ground next to her, I gave her the hooded sweatshirt and cup of water and asked if she was ok. Thankfully, I had my neighbor at my side for safety and as a witness. I could hardly get a word out of the girl, only her name and a few words that were hard to comprehend. When the girl looked at me, I could see the pain in her eyes that penetrated to the very depth of her heart, full of emptiness and despair.

She had a gospel tract from a local hospital, so I knew she was in search for hope. I asked her if she knew a man by the name of Jesus and the answer I got back was, "They did this to me." She then showed me her hand and arm that was full of needle marks. At that moment, I knew exactly what was going on, and God shared with me the revelation that pleasure will always have a price and cost at someone else's expense.

When her help arrived, it was a very spiritual experience; the person driving the car would not look me in the eye. **John 1:5** tells us, "…The light shines in the darkness, and the darkness did not comprehend it."

This was true looking into that man's eyes. He wanted nothing to do with me. We did call the authorities to let them know of the situation and to make sure that help was available to everyone. Looking at the situation, it seemed clear as **Isaiah 5:20** says, "Woe to those who call evil good, and good evil; who substitute darkness for light and light for darkness; who substitute bitter for sweet and sweet for bitter."

The girl now is in the proper care to guide her and help her recover where she can find hope and healing. I do ask that you join me in praying for this girl, that the Lord would protect her, and reveal Himself to her every day, that anything being formed against her would not succeed. If I had been watching a movie or playing a board game and enjoying time with these things, I wouldn't have been quiet enough to hear the Holy Spirit speaking to me to check on this girl and be a witness of Jesus' unconditional love and grace.

I am hoping that the day I get to see this girl again I will be able to call her a sister in the Kingdom of God, and get to hear of the amazing things the Lord has done in her life. I have faith that God is working in her life now.

I continue to think about all the chances we have every day to listen to the Holy Spirit and how He sets up appointments for us to witness the Good News of the gospels to the lost. I am in no way stating that watching a movie or playing a board game is wrong, or enjoying fun things with your family is wrong. The point I'm trying to get across is that God set this appointment up and allowed the quietness in my heart and mind so I could hear the call of the Holy Spirit.

Then we must be obedient, observant, and learn to recognize when God sets up these divine appointments set before us.

~*~

Lesson 2

Memory Verse:

Try your best to memorize the Biblical verse. It is ok to struggle with this as memorization can be difficult. Be sure to extend grace towards one another in memorizing Bible verses. This is to help create consistency and develop a good habit of thinking about Scripture throughout the day.

> *John 14:26:* "*But the Helper, the Holy Spirit, whom the Father will send in my name, He will teach you all things, and bring to your remembrance all that I said to you.*"

Before you share a quiet time with your group, be sure to pray that the Holy Spirit will guide you in your revelation of understanding and wisdom through the scriptures to share with your brothers. Share one quiet time with your group and how it applies to your daily life and walk as a believer.

Quiet Times:

Personal time of devotion and dedication, spending time in the Scriptures with the Lord.

John 14: 15-17 (Monday – Wednesday)

John 14: 23-26 (Thursday – Saturday)
Romans 8: 23-30 (Monday – Wednesday)
Isaiah 11: 2-4 (Thursday – Saturday)

During you quiet times, follow these guidelines and write them in a journal or notebook so you will be able to share your quiet time with your group. Share at least one quiet time with your group. Before sharing a quiet time, please begin by having one of your brothers pray over the group.

Quiet Time – Guideline:

- Be specific in your answers, writing a paragraph for each answer.
- Key point or theme of the passage/verse – What is the author's intent to the original audience?
- Key words – Repeated words in the text
- Emphasize word - Use a concordance or Bible dictionary to find what the context of the word means in your key verse.
- How will the application of the biblical principle make a difference in your daily walk with the Lord?
- Rewrite your key verse to make it personal to our modern time, without reading yourself into the text.
- How will this verse help you approach a lost person and tell them the love of Jesus?

- What is the original intent of the author to the original audience?
- Is there a biblical principle from the original audience we can apply in our modern time?
- What are the differences and similarities between the original audience and our modern audience?

Lesson 2 Discussion Questions:

Before answering this questions, please begin by praying for one another.

1. How has the Holy Spirit spoken to you? Was it a calling? Was it an answer to guidance and direction? How did this impact your daily walk?
2. Has there been a time when you felt the Holy Spirit tugging on your heart, but acted in disobedience? What was the effect of that decision?
3. When the Holy Spirit tugs at your heart both inside and outside of the church, how do you respond to the tug? What actions did you take to be obedient to the call of the Holy Spirit?
4. Has the Holy Spirit called you into a different scenario of life, career, place of residence, ministry, helping others? How have you responded to the call?

5. What is preventing you today from hearing the voice of the Holy Spirit? Why does this matter in your walk as a believer receiving the free gift of salvation?
6. How can hearing the voice of the Holy Spirit deepen your relationship with Jesus and win lost souls for Jesus in building His Kingdom?

The challenge for this week:

As you meditate on the Word through your quiet times, take a moment to be silent and just listen for the voice of the Holy Spirit.

Follow up:

Reach out to your brothers twice this week through text, phone call, email, face-to-face visit to encourage them in their walk; show them assurance of God's unconditional love.

Before you depart, pray for one another, encourage one another, ask for prayer needs throughout the week. Remember, the discussion of the questions above should lead to fellowship and not division. We come as brothers united in the Kingdom of God.

Exercise Plan – Week 3 and Week 4

Monday - chest
- Bench Press (4-5 sets, 15, 12, 10, 8 reps)
- Incline bench press (4-5 sets, 15, 12, 10, 8 reps)
- Dumbbell flyes (4-5 sets, 15, 12, 10, 8 reps)
- Cable cross (4-5 sets, 15, 12, 10, 8 reps)
- ` Chest press (4-5 sets, 15, 12, 10, 8 reps)
- Dips (4-5 sets, 15, 12, 10, 8 reps)
- 20 minutes cardio – seated row, jog, run, elliptical, bike riding

Tuesday – back and abs
- Deadlift (4-5 sets, 15, 12, 10, 8 reps)
- Lat pulldown (4-5 sets, 15, 12, 10, 8 reps)
- Lat half-moon (4-5 sets, 15, 12, 10, 8 reps)
- Machine rows (4-5 sets, 15, 12, 10, 8 reps)
- Dumbbell rows (4-5 sets, 15, 12, 10, 8 reps)
- Weighted crunches (4-5 sets, 15, 12, 10, 8 reps)
- 20 minutes cardio – seated row, jog, run, elliptical, bike riding

Wednesday – shoulders and traps
- Front to back military press (4-5 sets, 15, 12, 10, 8 reps)
- Front raises (4-5 sets, 15, 12, 10, 8 reps)

- Lateral raises (4-5 sets, 15, 12, 10, 8 reps)
- Shrugs (4-5 sets, 15, 12, 10, 8 reps)
- Delt flyes (4-5 sets, 15, 12, 10, 8 reps)
- Rear delt raises (4-5 sets, 15, 12, 10, 8 reps)
- 20 minutes cardio – seated row, jog, run, elliptical, bike riding

Thursday – arms
- Bicep curls (4-5 sets, 15, 12, 10, 8 reps)
- Barbell curls (4-5 sets, 15, 12, 10, 8 reps)
- Preacher curls (4-5 sets, 15, 12, 10, 8 reps)
- Hammer curls (4-5 sets, 15, 12, 10, 8 reps)
- Triceps pushdown (4-5 sets, 15, 12, 10, 8 reps)
- Skull crusher (4-5 sets, 15, 12, 10, 8 reps)
- Triceps extension (4-5 sets, 15, 12, 10, 8 reps)
- Dumbbell kickbacks (4-5 sets, 15, 12, 10, 8 reps)
- 20 minutes cardio – seated row, jog, run, elliptical, bike riding

Friday – legs
- Squats (4-5 sets, 15, 12, 10, 8 reps)
- Leg press (4-5 sets, 15, 12, 10, 8 reps)
- Leg extension (4-5 sets, 15, 12, 10, 8 reps)
- Leg curls (4-5 sets, 15, 12, 10, 8 reps)
- Stiff-leg deadlift (4-5 sets, 15, 12, 10, 8 reps)
- Lunges (4-5 sets, 15, 12, 10, 8 reps)

- Sitting Calf raises (4-5 sets, 15, 12, 10, 8 reps)
- 20 minutes cardio – seated row, jog, run, elliptical, bike riding

Saturday and Sunday – Recovery

As you rest and recover, be sure your family is always a priority. Your family also comes before the regular exercise routine during the week. It is far more important and valuable that you are spiritually leading your family than spending countless hours at the gym or exercising in your home gym. The exercise routine is to help you see measurable results as you go through the study each week. Be intentional with your family and help develop, build, and grow them spiritually, getting to Jesus in a deeper way…

3

ANSWERING THE CALL FROM THE LORD

One of the most confusing times a believer can have is when they feel called by the Lord. There are many different callings that the Lord gives to someone, which is why this should not be taken lightly. We should diligently seek the Lord without hesitation when we feel a call from Him. We should never try to create the calling or so-called opportunity on our own strength. If we do this, we are placing ourselves above God, which is wholly prohibited when hearing and understanding the true call from the Lord.

I have seen many pastors who say they have felt called to preach from the pulpit, yet there was no confirmation; they created the opportunity through a degree and filled a needed position. This has also happened with missionaries. When this happens, the power of the Holy Spirit and the presence of the Holy

Spirit can not only be grieved but also extinguished, bearing a fruitless ministry.

Before we can understand and hear the call of the Lord, we need to do our due diligence and weed out the things that cause separation between us and God's Word. This can be a painful process at times, as the flesh wants to stay grounded in the world, yet our spirits long to be in Heaven. I think Ephesians does a beautiful job explaining this. **Ephesians 2:1-3** says, "And you were dead in the trespasses and sins in which you once walked, following the course of this world, following the prince of the power of the air, the spirit that is now at work in the sons of disobedience, (3) among whom we all once lived in the passions of our flesh, carrying out the desires of the body and the mind, and were by nature children of wrath, like the rest of mankind. (ESV). Through this verse, we see how a simple desire of the mind or flesh can clog our ears and give us a spiritual cataract, instead of pointing us toward Jesus. We must come to the realization that even though we are very much alive physically, we are dead spiritually.

When we come to this realization, we can clearly see and hear the call from the Lord and the direction and guidance of the Holy Spirit. So, how do we hear the calling of the Lord? For us to hear His voice, we must have faith. At our conversion, we received spiritual life from the One who gave us life, Jesus. A very clear and straightforward example of hearing the call of the Lord is demonstrated through the experience of Lazarus and Jesus. John 11 shows us this example in a very intimate and faith-driven way. **John 11:40-43** tells us Jesus said to her:

"'Did I not say to you that of you believe you would see the glory of God?' (41) Then they took away the stone from the place where the dead man was lying. And Jesus lifted up His eyes and said, 'Father, I thank you that you have heard Me. (42) And I know the you always hear Me, but because of the people who are standing by I said this, that they may believe that You sent Me.' (43) Now when He had said these things, He cried with a loud voice, 'Lazarus, come forth!' (44) And he who had died came out bound hand and foot with graveclothes, and his face was wrapped with a cloth. Jesus said to them, 'Loose him, and let him go'" (ESV).

Think for a moment about the state of Lazarus: He was dead, in complete silence, nothing distracting his physical body, in a quiet, dark tomb. The stillness and silence of the tomb allowed his spirit to listen to the call of the Lord. We also see that when Jesus called to the Father, He had faith that the Father was listening, and Jesus didn't question it for a single second. We must also have this same faith, not only when praying to the Father, but also when hearing His voice when He calls.

The importance of being still and listening is serious. Through this, we see that Jesus didn't allow emotions to be in front of His faith, and emotions had no way of interfering with Lazarus hearing the call and voice of the Lord.

Now, Jesus did have emotions before he called Lazarus in one of the saddest verses in the Word of God. We see it in **John 11:3:** "Jesus wept." Jesus allowed His emotions to come forth before calling out to Lazarus. Similarly, when we pray and ask God for guidance, we must allow our emotions to settle before we can hear the call from the Lord.

If we do not rid ourselves of the emotions first, they can twist, taint, distort, manipulate, and even give a false sense of hope. We need to make sure we are hearing clearly and in faith. If we come to the Lord with requests, we need to come to Him clearly in order to hear His call. **Proverbs 27:19** tells us, (29) "…as in water face reflects face, so the heart of man reflects man." We must always be sure that our emotions do not get in the way of communicating with the Lord and hearing from Him. We must also allow the examination process to happen before we can truly hear and recognize the call of the Lord.

In **Psalm 26:2** we are told in the Psalm "(2) Examine me, O Lord, and try me; Test my mind and my heart." When we allow this proving to take place, we can separate emotions that try to tell us our calling, from knowing and believing the call the Lord has given us. We must leave room for clear communication between us and the Lord.

When it comes to hearing the call from the Lord, I have noticed multiple things come to mind that we must consider and think about: First, is the call only for you personally? Second, is the call to put others' interests first? Third, is there confirmation of this calling from the Lord? Fourth, has this calling led you to prayer and searching the Word for guidance?

Many people quickly state that they have been called by the Lord to do something. The negative part is that most could not honestly answer the four questions here. There is usually a hint of pride and selfishness in their call, which explains why it can be destructive to allow emotions to be part of hearing the voice of the Lord.

In my personal experience, when I have felt the calling, and heard the voice of the Lord, I can answer those four questions. **Philippians 2:4** explains the answer to one of the questions, stating to not merely look out for your own interests, but also for the interests of others. It is pretty clear that a calling from the Lord will also involve other people. We must love others, **1 John 4:7-8** says, "Dear friends, let us love one another, for love comes from God. Everyone who loves has been born of God and knows God. Whoever does not love does not know God because God is love" (ESV, 2024).

Through love, we cast out all selfishness and pride because God is Love. With Love, we will not conform to the ways of this world, which would hinder us from hearing the voice of God. **Romans 12:2** tells us, "…do not conform to the pattern of this world but be transformed by renewing your mind. Then you can test and approve what God's will is – His good, pleasing and perfect will." (CSB, 2022)

When we hear the call from the Lord, we must always be giving thanks and praise to Him for this call. **Psalm 107:1, 8-9** says**,** "Give thanks to the Lord, for He is good, for His mercy is everlasting". (8-9) "They shall give thanks to the Lord for His mercy, and for His wonders to the sons of mankind! For He has satisfied the thirsty soul, and He has filled the hungry soul with what is good."

~*~

Lesson 3

Memory Verse:
Try your best to memorize the Biblical verse. It is ok to struggle with this as memorization can be difficult. Be sure to extend grace towards one another in memorizing Bible verses. This is to help create consistency and develop a good habit of thinking about Scripture throughout the day.

> ***Psalm 9:1:*** *"I will give thanks to the Lord with all my heart; I will tell of all Your wonders."*

Quiet Times:
Personal time of devotion and dedication, spending time in the Scriptures with the Lord.
John 11: 40-43 (Monday – Wednesday)
Romans 12: 2-5 (Thursday – Saturday)
Psalm 26: 1-7 (Monday – Wednesday)
Need one more (Thursday – Saturday)

During you quiet times follow these guidelines and write them in a journal or notebook so you will be able to share your quiet time with your group. Share at least one quiet time with your group. Before sharing a quiet time, please begin by having one of your brothers pray over the group.

Quiet Time – Guideline:
- Be specific in your answers, writing a paragraph for each answer.
- Key point or theme of the passage/verse – What is the author's intent to the original audience?
- Key Words – Repeated words in the text
- Emphasize word - Use a concordance or Bible dictionary to find what the context of the word means in your key verse.
- How will the application of the biblical principle make a difference in your daily walk with the Lord?
- Rewrite your key verse to make it personal to our modern time, without reading yourself into the text.
- How will this verse help you approach a lost person and tell them about the love of Jesus?
- What is the original intent of the author to the original audience?
- Is there a biblical principle from the original audience we can apply in our modern time?
- What are the differences and similarities between the original audience and our modern audience?

Lesson 3 Discussion Questions:

Be prepared to share and converse over the answered questions from Lesson 3 with your group. Remember to keep this dialogue productive and pointed toward the Lord exalting His name on High.

1. When in your daily walk have you felt the calling of the Lord? How was the calling from the Lord revealed to you?
2. Have you had confirmation with the calling that the Lord has placed on your heart? Have you spent time in prayer over this calling?
3. In what areas has the Lord called you to serve and take the interests of other before your own interests?
4. Has there ever been a time when you allowed pride and selfishness to dilute and repel you from hearing the call from the Lord?
5. What changes have or will you make in your daily walk so you hear the call of the Lord? How will this reflect your obedience to being in the Word daily?
6. Have there been any struggles, pains, divisions, materials, forms of entertainment, or other factors that have distanced you from hearing the call of the Lord through His Word? What actions will you take, so that you can hear the call clearly?

Before departing your group, go around the group and pray for one another. This week be sure to reach out once to everyone in your group to see how they are doing with the action steps provided in the questions from this lesson. Be sure to encourage your brothers in their walks, and always show the example of unconditional love, just as our Father in Heaven has shown us.

Exercise Plan – Week 5 and Week 6

Monday

- DB side lateral raises - 5 set x 12, 10, 10, 10, 8/16, 8/16
- Barbell squat – 5 set x 12, 10, 10, 10, 8/16, 8/16
- Leg extensions – 5 set x 12, 10, 10, 10, 8/16, 8/16
- Leg curls – 5 set x 12, 10, 10, 10, 8/16, 8/16
- 20 minutes of cardio – seated row, jog, run, elliptical, bike riding, swimming

Tuesday

- Seated DB presses - 4 x 12, 12, 10,8/16
- Seated bent over rear delt raises - 4 x 12, 12, 10/20, 10/20
- Cable side raises - 4 x 12, 12, 10, 10 Cable in front of the body or behind.
- DB front raises - 4 x 12, 12, 10, 10/10/10 Last set is a drop set. Decrease the weight each time by 5-10lbs and continue to get 10 reps until you can no longer get 10 reps.
- Shrugs with DB - 6-8 sets x Failure (use a weight that is within 80-85% of your max rep)

- 20 minutes cardio – seated row, jog, run, elliptical, bike riding, swimming

Wednesday
- Bent-over dumbbell row – 4x 12, 12, 10, 8/20
- One-arm dumbbell row – 4x 12, 12, 10, 8/20
- Wide-grip lat pulldown – 4x 12, 12, 10, 8/20
- Standing dumbbell triceps extension – 4x 15, 15, 12, 10/20
- 20 minutes cardio – seated row, jog, run, elliptical, bike riding, swimming

Thursday – Sunday

This time is intentionally reserved for family time. Do something active with your family like going for a walk, biking on trails, playing outdoor games in the back yard, or whatever time of enjoyment which brings fulfillment to your heart. This will help you to recognize the gift God has given you with your family.

4

Applying the Word to Our Actions

James 1:22 tells us, "But be doers of the word and not hearers only, deceiving yourselves." It is common in the church body today that a majority are only hearers of the Word, leaving our Christian experience in the four walls of the church. We are called to apply what we know about the Word of God. If we are not doers, we quickly find ourselves being deceived by our own emotions and perspectives which can be a tool that the enemy uses to attack us in our daily walk being that our battle is not against flesh and blood, but by the spiritual forces around us that try to distort and manipulate the truth of God's Word trying to encourage individuals to follow the ways of the world.

Ephesians 6:12 tells us, "…for our struggle is not against flesh and blood, but against the rulers, against the powers, against the world forces of this darkness, against the spiritual forces of wickedness in the heavenly places." If we are slow to not only apply what we hear, but also see in the Word of God, it is easy to see how we can be deceived and manipulated. Part of our Christian experience and walk as doers of the Word is to be a good witness for the Kingdom of God.

When we are not actively putting the Word of God into action, we find ourselves on a slow fade to a dull and stagnant faith and Christian experience. This means we are not in the Word daily, we are not praying, our outreach is minimal, and our encouragement of the church body is limited. From here, selfishness and pride can creep in like a thief in the night, ready to devour us at any given moment. At this moment, we may truly find ourselves in a situation that can lead to declining faith and psychological damage to other believers.

It is essential that we are doers of the Word, as stated in James 1:22, to help build one another up. Our church body attends the church because it is our spiritual hospital that is much needed. If we only listen to the Word, we fail to see the power, mercy, grace and love behind the good works that God has called us to do.

Remember that everything a Christian does hinges on the truth of the death and resurrection of Jesus Christ. These completed acts by Jesus Christ demonstrate to a fallen world the unconditional love, grace, and mercy, which testify truth to Jesus Christ's character.

So, how do we become doers of the Word and not just listeners who are easily deceived? We need to start with self-discipline and self-control. **James 1:19** tells us, '…This you know, my beloved brethren. But everyone must be quick to hear, slow to speak and slow to anger." By applying **James 1:19**, we can now fully engage our church body and the lost with understanding, not emotionality. **Titus 2:2** tells us that older men are to be sober-minded, dignified, self-controlled, sound in faith, in love, and in steadfastness.

When we take it a step further in **Romans 8:13,** where we are told, "…for if you live according to the flesh, you must die; but if by the Spirit you are putting to death the deeds of the body, you will live." Part of self-control has to do with self-examination and self-reflection; this is the point at which we see if we are putting others above ourselves or ourselves above others. If we always view ourselves above others, we get trapped in our mind, which leads us away from being doers and possibly not even listeners.

Thinking of self-discipline can be challenging for anyone as we face ourselves in the mirror, looking at the need for repentance and forgiveness. This is where we see the dirt and grit of who we were before we knew Jesus as our Lord and Savior. When we face reality and start implementing self-discipline, we allow the Holy Spirit to come in and clean the house. Self-discipline helps us build a healthy habit of being in the Word daily and having a daily prayer life. This can only happen with the renewing of the mind daily.

Ephesians 4:23-24 says that you are "to be renewed in the spirit of your minds, and to put on the new self, the one created according to God's likeness in righteousness and purity of the truth" (CSB). This keeps our hearts and minds centered on Christ, who can give us guidance through His Holy Spirit. When this takes place, we find ourselves at a point where we not only can listen to the word, but also apply it with action. This is needed daily; otherwise, we chance jeopardizing our witness and reaching a loss.

Another point to touch on is that by applying the Word to our actions, we can begin to engage in spiritual warfare and have victory over our daily battles. I'm sure you know someone—or even yourself—who is constantly worn down from the daily attacks from our enemy. Spiritual warfare can be draining emotionally, physically, and spiritually. However, once we learn how to apply the Word to our daily lives, we start operating under the power of the Holy Spirit that was given to us. This is the same power that raised Jesus from the grave.

Ephesians 1:20-22 tells us "…He exercised this power in Christ by raising Him from the dead and seating him at His right hand in the heavens – far above every ruler and authority, power and dominion, and every title given, not only in this age but also in the one to come. And He subjected everything under His feet and appointed Him as head over everything for the church."

Before I understood how vital self-control and self-discipline were in my daily walk, I felt like all I was doing was wandering around aimlessly. I was always giving into temptation and being defeated by battle. I had very impulsive behavior and a personality to match, which are completely opposite of control and discipline. I was still immature, and even though I was considered an adult by age, I very much had a youthful mind that wanted to go astray. It's easy to see and understand now why there wasn't more victory back then as a young believer.

Even though I did believe in Jesus and what He did on the cross for me, I was still in my old habits. I didn't understand that I needed a complete character change, and until that character change came, there was no way I could apply the Word to my daily life. I needed to have self-control and self-discipline to understand the Word and know how to apply the Word. I never really knew the value of those two characteristics until I got older. They are extremely important and a key point to living out a life of holiness and godliness that would align with the will of God.

As you begin to practice self-control and self-discipline, the enemy will surely attack you. It will always be essential to be understanding and keep on moving forward. If you look in the rearview mirror, you will never see what lies ahead. Be prepared to help encourage your brothers as they start and continue to practice these key characteristics of the Christian walk. Then they can also apply the Word to their daily walk, living out the Word and being an example for the lost. This will help us in our witness, align our hearts with God's will, and exalt the name of Jesus on high.

LESSON 4

Memory Verse:

Try your best to memorize the Biblical verse. It is ok to struggle with this as memorization can be difficult. Be sure to extend grace towards one another in memorizing Bible verses. This is to help create consistency and develop a good habit of thinking about Scripture throughout the day.

> ***James 1:22:*** *"But prove yourselves doers of the word, and not merely hearers who delude themselves."*

Quiet Times:

Personal time of devotion and dedication, spending time in the Scriptures with the Lord.
Ephesians 1:20-22 (Monday – Wednesday)
Ephesians 4:23-24 (Thursday – Saturday)
Romans 8:13-16 (Monday – Wednesday)
Ephesians 6:12-13 (Thursday – Saturday)

During you quiet times follow these guidelines and write them in a journal or notebook so you will be able to share your quiet time with your group. Share at least one quiet time with your group. Before sharing a quiet time, please begin by having one of your brothers pray over the group.

Quiet Time – Guideline:

- Be specific in your answers, writing a paragraph for each answer.
- Key point or theme of the passage/verse – What is the author's intent to the original audience?
- Key Words – Repeated words in the text
- Emphasize word - Use a concordance or Bible dictionary to find what the context of the word means in your key verse.
- How will the application of the biblical principle make a difference in your daily walk with the Lord?
- Rewrite your key verse to make it personal to our modern time, without reading yourself into the text.
- How will this verse help you approach a lost person and tell them about the love of Jesus?
- What is the original intent of the author to the original audience?
- Is there a biblical principle from the original audience we can apply in our modern time?

- What are the differences and similarities between the original audience and our modern audience?

Lesson 4 Discussion Questions:

Before answering the questions as a group, pray for the guidance of your conversation and leading from the Holy Spirit.

1. What are your interpretation and perspective on self-discipline and self-control? How do these two characteristics look in the believer and the non-believer? What is the distinguishing factor that can lead to victory for the believer?
2. What areas of your daily walk require self-examination to be able to demonstrate self-control and self-discipline, so that your witness to both believers and non-believers will be true and faithful?
3. When was the last time you let an impulsive action take over the key characteristics of self-control and self-discipline? What was the outcome and how were you able to correct this and make it right?
4. Is there an area in your daily walk now where your brothers can help guide, direct, support and encourage you? If so, what actions will you ask of your brothers to help build you?

DEVELOPING A DISCIPLE

5. How will you help your brothers when they are feeling down and defeated by the attacks of the enemy? What is your follow up plan through the week to make sure everyone is staying in unity and not breaking apart? How will this help deepen your brotherly relationship?
6. Do you know someone now who has thought about Jesus but has never really accepted the Word of his unfailing love? With self-control and self-discipline, how can you approach them this week to be a witness of what Jesus has done in your life? What will this mean to the lost person, and what difference can it make in their life?

Before you depart form the group, pray over the discussion you just had. Make it a point to follow up with you brothers this week and check in with them. This could be a phone call, text, visit, coffee shop, lunch, but commit to follow up so that you may sharpen yourselves and know how to pray for each other and your families.

The battle is real. We must be watchful. We must apply God's Word daily to live in victory.

Exercise Plan – Week 5 and Week 6

Monday

- DB side lateral raises - 5 set x 12, 10, 10, 10, 8/16, 8/16
- Barbell squat – 5 set x 12, 10, 10, 10, 8/16, 8/16
- Leg extensions – 5 set x 12, 10, 10, 10, 8/16, 8/16
- Leg curls – 5 set x 12, 10, 10, 10, 8/16, 8/16
- 20 minutes of cardio – seated row, jog, run, elliptical, bike riding, swimming

Tuesday

- Seated DB presses - 4 x 12, 12, 10, 8/16
- Seated bent over rear delt raises - 4 x 12, 12, 10/20, 10/20
- Cable side raises - 4 x 12, 12, 10, 10 Cable in front of the body or behind.
- DB Front Raises - 4 x 12, 12, 10, 10/10/10 Last set is a drop set. Decrease the weight each time by 5-10lbs and continue to get 10 reps until you can no longer get 10 reps.
- Shrugs with DB - 6-8 sets x Failure (use a weight that is within 80-85% of your max rep)
- 20 minutes cardio – seated row, jog, run, elliptical, bike riding, swimming

Wednesday

- Bent-over dumbbell row – 4x 12, 12, 10, 8/20
- One-arm dumbbell row – 4x 12, 12, 10, 8/20
- Wide-grip lat pulldown – 4x 12, 12, 10, 8/20
- Standing dumbbell triceps extension – 4x 15, 15, 12, 10/20
- 20 minutes cardio – seated row, jog, run, elliptical, bike riding, swimming

Thursday – Sunday

This time is intentionally reserved for family time. Do something active with your family, like going for a walk, biking on trails, playing outdoor games in the back yard. This time should be an enjoyable fulfillment to your heart, to recognize the gift God has given you with your family.

5

KNOWING WHAT SOIL WE ARE WORKING WITH

When it comes to witnessing, evangelizing, and outreach in or outside of the church, it will be important to understand the soil you will be working with. A farmer knows the soil he works with so that he may correctly plant a seed that will soon grow into something beautiful to be harvested. It seems that many individuals in the modern church go through seasons of their walk in different soil. The challenge is to remain consistent in becoming fertile soil. Fertile soil then produces good fruit which will give a true testimony of what God can do to the human heart.

There are many types of soil that we work with daily: fertile, sterile, rocky, muddy, sandy, and saturated, to name just a few. Knowing how to discern what type of soil a person represents can be very challenging. We have to rely on discernment from the Holy Spirit. **Malachi 3:18** says, "So you will again distinguish between the righteous and the wicked, between one who serves God and one who does not serve Him." As we discern what soil types we are working with, we also have to take account of our own soil to make sure we are approaching people in a way that honors God and His Kingdom. **Job 34:4** says, "…let us choose for ourselves what is right; let us understand among ourselves what is good." If we don't discern their soil, we can be misleading and manipulative in our approach to helping our brothers or reaching the lost. Everything we do needs to honor God and His word.

Even though there are many types of soil, all these soils make up one field. **Matthew 13:38** says, "and the field is the world; and as for the good seed, these are the sons of the kingdom; and the weeds are the sons of the evil one." The weeds are the sons of the evil one or those who serve the world and reject the truth and light of God's Word. The soil in the field of the world allows either plants or weeds to grow. Knowing the soil you are working with will help you to plant the correct seed. As with a farmer in a field, there is always a different approach to working the soil so that it will accept the seed that is about to be planted. We must take the same approach when thinking about witnessing to other people. We need to understand what type of soil a person represents so that we may adequately plant the seed in their heart.

Matthew 13:20 gives us a perfect example of rocky soil, and as for what was sown on rocky ground, this is the one who hears the word and immediately receives it with joy. Think about that verse and notice that rocks can be removed from the soil. Even though some require more work, there is still fertile soil. After the rocks are removed, the soil is left fertile to have seeds planted and watered to host a beautiful crop to harvest.

I have noticed many times in my personal Christian experience that most of those in outreach or evangelism don't discern the soil that they are about to begin working with. This can be a very disappointing and discouraging time for a believer. You work hard but see no results of your efforts. The seed never takes hold, never grows, never gets watered, and cannot be harvested. Now, some of this has to do with people operating under their own strength and power, rather than letting the power of Jesus operate and work. But for the simple case of working with soil, this is a good example.

As we spend more time in the Word and apply the Word to our actions, it will become easier to discern different soil types and know how to work the ground (heart). As we discern different types of soil, we really discern the heart. When this happens, we are able to see the emptiness in the lost soul that so desperately needs to hear the Word. We also see where the lost stand regarding loving darkness more than the light of truth that we read daily. **John 3:20** states "…for everyone who does evil hates the Light, and does not come to the Light for fear that his deeds will be exposed." Also in **Mark 7:21-22,** it says, "For from within, out of the heart of men, proceed evil the thoughts, fornications, thefts, murders, adulteries, deeds of coveting and wickedness, as well as deceit, sensuality, envy, slander, pride and foolishness."

These verses are perfect examples of different soil types and why we must discern and know the soil we are working with. It is the only way to know how to break down the heart and soften it so it can accept the Word of truth and the light that comes from it. When we know the soil we are working with, we realize how to plant a seed and water it. Once the seed is planted, then the Holy Spirit is able to cultivate and nourish the seed within the soil where it was planted.

It's easy to become irritated, frustrated, and even angry when speaking to someone who has soil that is different from our own. It can often be portrayed as though they are not listening to us, they don't care, and we ask ourselves, *why don't they understand what I'm saying?* When these feelings come up, it puts us in as much danger as any of the soil types mentioned in **Mark 7:21-22**. With these emotions, pride and selfishness can easily sneak in and change our motives and intentions without us knowing. We need to be diligent in our approach to working with soil and commit all we do to the Lord; that way, the Lord is the one working the soil, only using us as a vessel.

To go a step further, there are soil types and issues not only in the non-believer but also in the believer. I've seen it on multiple occasions where a conversation on the Word will take place, but before you know it, it has turned into a heated theological argument between two people trying to prove their intellectual ability to understand the Word of God on a higher level than the other person. Honestly, what does that accomplish? Absolutely nothing! If one of the two people would have sat back and remained calm and patient, they could have discerned the soil type and had a constructive and productive conversation that glorified the Word and our Lord Jesus.

Knowing and understanding what soil we are working with is a must for all believers to have a fulfilling Christian experience. It is one of the ways we not only know how to reach the lost, but also how to build and encourage other believers. Discerning soil types takes time, so be patient with yourself; always look to the Word, and ask God to allow His Holy Spirit to guide and direct you.

The life of a believer is a lifelong journey, just like our testimony; it never ends. God is always doing something, and He is always deserving praise, thanksgiving, honor, worship, and full submission to Him from His believers. So be patient, work on God's timing and not your own, and always give thanks and praise. Then, you will be able to discern and work with different soil types.

Lesson 5

Memory Verse:

Try your best to memorize the Biblical verse. It is ok to struggle with this as memorization can be difficult. Be sure to extend grace towards one another in memorizing Bible verses. This is to help create consistency and develop a good habit of thinking about Scripture throughout the day.

> ***Matthew 13:20***: *"The one on whom seed was sown on the rocky places, this is the man who hears the word and immediately receives it with joy."*

Quiet Times:

Personal time of devotion and dedication, spending time in the Scriptures with the Lord.

Mark 7:21-22 (Monday – Wednesday)
John 3:16-21 (Thursday – Saturday)
Job 34:2-6 (Monday – Wednesday)
Malachi 3:16-18 (Thursday – Saturday)

During you quiet times follow these guidelines and write them in a journal or notebook so that you will be able to share your quiet time with your group. Share at least one quiet time with your group. Before sharing a

quiet time, please begin by having one of your brothers pray over the group.

Quiet Time – Guideline:

- Be specific in your answers, writing a paragraph for each answer.
- Key point or theme of the passage/verse – What is the author's intent to the original audience?
- Key Words – Repeated words in the text
- Emphasize word - Use a concordance or Bible dictionary to find what the context of the word means in your key verse.
- What is the original intent of the author to the original audience?
- Is there a biblical principle from the original audience we can apply in our modern time?
- How will the application of the biblical principle make a difference in your daily walk with the Lord?
- Rewrite your key verse to make it personal to our modern time, without reading yourself into the text.
- How will this verse help you approach a lost person and tell them the love of Jesus?
- What are the differences and similarities between the original audience and our modern audience?

Lesson 5 Discussion Questions:

Be ready to share your answers to the questions from Lesson 5 with your group. Remember to be an example of patience, kindness, love, mercy, and grace while listening to your brothers' answers from this lesson.

1. Has the Word of God revealed the type of soil you are working with? What type is the soil, and how does it affect your daily walk with God?
2. Have you ever had difficulty discerning what type of soil you are working with to reach the lost? How did this affect your faith? What were the results and consequences that came about?
3. What actions can you take to understand what soil type you are working with? Why does the soil type matter when trying to soften a heart to accept the Word of truth?
4. How will you help ensure you and your brothers always have fertile soil to share with others? What steps and actions will you take to develop trust, love, and a deeper relationship so you can remove rocks when they come up out of the soil?
5. Is there anything now that would be considered a rock or weed in your soil that needs to be removed so you can help your brothers and share the Good News with others? If so, how

will you allow your brothers to help build and encourage you?

6. What is needed to understand soil types? Why is this important for the believer, and how will you apply this to your daily walk?

7. Are all soils good soil? Explain your answer with evidence from the Word. Be sure to list books, chapters and verses you use.

Before parting ways, pray with your group. One person takes the lead this time and prays over the entire group. Encourage one another before departing.

Exercise Plan – Week 9 and Week 10

Monday - chest
- Bench press (4-5 sets, 15, 12, 10, 8 reps)
- Incline bench press (4-5 sets, 15, 12, 10, 8 reps)
- Dumbbell press (4-5 sets, 15, 12, 10, 8 reps)
- Dumbbell flyes (4-5 sets, 15, 12, 10, 8 reps)
- Cable cross (4-5 sets, 15, 12, 10, 8 reps)
- Chest press (4-5 sets, 15, 12, 10, 8 reps)
- Dips (4-5 sets, 15, 12, 10, 8 reps)
- 20 minutes cardio – seated row, jog, run, elliptical, bike riding

Tuesday – back and abs
- Deadlift (4-5 sets, 15, 12, 10, 8 reps)
- Lat pulldown (4-5 sets, 15, 12, 10, 8 reps)
- Lat half-moon (4-5 sets, 15, 12, 10, 8 reps)
- Machine rows (4-5 sets, 15, 12, 10, 8 reps)
- Dumbbell rows (4-5 sets, 15, 12, 10, 8 reps)
- Weighted crunches (4-5 sets, 15, 12, 10, 8 reps)
- Leg raises (4-5 sets, 15, 12, 10, 8 reps)
- Sit-ups (4-5 sets, 15, 12, 10, 8 reps)
- 20 minutes cardio – seated row, jog, run, elliptical, bike riding

Wednesday – shoulders and traps

- Front to back military press (4-5 sets, 15, 12, 10, 8 reps)
- Arnold press (4-5 sets, 15, 12, 10, 8 reps)
- Front raises (4-5 sets, 15, 12, 10, 8 reps)
- Lateral raises (4-5 sets, 15, 12, 10, 8 reps)
- Shrugs (4-5 sets, 15, 12, 10, 8 reps)
- Delt flyes (4-5 sets, 15, 12, 10, 8 reps)
- Rear delt raises (4-5 sets, 15, 12, 10, 8 reps)
- 20 minutes cardio – seated row, jog, run, elliptical, bike riding

Thursday – arms

- Bicep curls (4-5 sets, 15, 12, 10, 8 reps)
- Barbell curls (4-5 sets, 15, 12, 10, 8 reps)
- Preacher curls (4-5 sets, 15, 12, 10, 8 reps)
- Hammer curls (4-5 sets, 15, 12, 10, 8 reps)
- Triceps pushdown (4-5 sets, 15, 12, 10, 8 reps)
- Triceps dips (4-5 sets, 15, 12, 10, 8 reps)
- Skull crusher (4-5 sets, 15, 12, 10, 8 reps)
- Triceps extension (4-5 sets, 15, 12, 10, 8 reps)
- Dumbbell kickbacks (4-5 sets, 15, 12, 10, 8 reps)
- 20 minutes cardio – seated row, jog, run, elliptical, bike riding

Friday – legs
- Squats (4-5 sets, 15, 12, 10, 8 reps)
- Leg press (4-5 sets, 15, 12, 10, 8 reps)
- Leg extension (4-5 sets, 15, 12, 10, 8 reps)
- Leg curls (4-5 sets, 15, 12, 10, 8 reps)
- Stiff-leg deadlift (4-5 sets, 15, 12, 10, 8 reps)
- Lunges (4-5 sets, 15, 12, 10, 8 reps)
- Sitting Calf raises (4-5 sets, 15, 12, 10, 8 reps)
- Standing calf raises (4-5 sets, 15, 12, 10, 8 reps)
- Donkey calf raises (4-5 sets, 15, 12, 10, 8 reps)
- 20 minutes cardio – seated row, jog, run, elliptical, bike riding

Saturday and Sunday – Recovery

As you rest and recover, be sure your family is always a priority. Your family also comes before the regular exercise routine during the week. It is far more important and valuable that you are spiritually leading your family than spending countless hours at the gym or exercising in your home gym. The exercise routine is to help you see measurable results as you go through the study each week. Be intentional with your family and help develop, build, and grow them spiritually, getting to Jesus in a deeper way.

6

KNOWING OUR STRENGTH IN JESUS

Having a solid understanding of our strength in Jesus will help us maintain a life of victory that honors God and His kingdom, rather than living in defeat. **Philippians 2:12-13** states, "…so then, my beloved, just as you have always obeyed, not as in my presence only, but now much more in my absence, work out your salvation with fear and trembling; for it is God who is at work in you, both to will and to work for his good pleasure."

Knowing our strength in Jesus is vital to our daily walk as Christians and the success we see in helping build the Kingdom of God. There is no other place where we can find strength, especially in ourselves. When we look for strength outside of the Word of God, we can find ourselves led astray and distracted. We can reassure ourselves of the strength we have in

Jesus by reading and meditating on the Word of God, which is why we need to renew our minds daily.

This not only leads to strength, but also to a life of obedience so we can live in God's will that He has for our lives. There are several passages that show us the strength we have in our Lord. **Psalm 46: 1-3** tells us, "God is our refuge and strength, a helper who is always found in times of trouble. Therefore we will not be afraid, though the earth trembles and the mountains topple into the seas, though its water roars and foams and the mountains quake with its turmoil" (CSB, 2022). Again, in **Exodus 15:2** we see, "The Lord is my strength and my song; he has become my salvation. This is my God, and I will praise Him – my father's God, and I will exalt Him" (CSB, 2022). I do believe we see that we can trust that there is strength in Jesus, and by trusting, we will begin to know our strength in Jesus.

I have noticed many times as people begin to think about strength, it always goes back to thinking about physical strength, like a weight lifter in a gym. There is rarely a thought about spiritual strength, even less a thought about joy being strength, which joy comes from the Lord. **Nehemiah 8:10** says, "…Do not grieve, for the joy of the Lord is your strength" (CSB, 2022).

Nehemiah describes perfectly how joy can overcome fear, oppression, depression, anger and many other things. There is a lot of strength in joy, which only comes from the Lord. However, before we have this kind of joy that has a solid sense of strength, we need to seek and take refuge in Jesus.

Two verses come to mind that represent this clearly. **Psalm 34:10** states, "Young lions lack food and go hungry, but those who seek the Lord will not lack any good thing" (CSB, 2022). Again, in **Psalm 9:9-10** we learn, "The Lord is a refuge for the persecuted, a refuge in times of trouble. Those who know your name trust in you because you have not abandoned those who seek you, Lord."

We have assurance in these two verses that by seeking the Lord we can receive joy to overcome a multitude of attacks and issues we face daily. As we walk through daily life being pulled in every direction, easily distracted, and tempted on every level, when we ask Jesus for joy, we know that He goes before us and will not fail us. **Deuteronomy 31:8** says, "The Lord is the one who goes ahead of you; He will be with you. He will not fail you or forsake you. Do not fear or be dismayed."

Something as small as joy assures us that the Lord is always with us. As we trust and exercise our faith, knowing Jesus is always with us, we find our strength in Him alone. It is overwhelming to think that Jesus is always with us and, at the same time, peaceful, knowing He is always there; we know we do not need to rely on our own strength, but on the strength that can only come from Him. There is victory when we allow Jesus to go before us and we rely on His strength.

So many times in my life, I tried to rely on my own strength, not knowing my real strength in Jesus. Part of this was due to not having a complete and total surrender to the Lord in every area of my life. I do believe that not surrendering fully can lead to spiritual blindness that hinders us from seeing the strength we have in Jesus. Once I became fully submitted and surrendered in every area of life, I felt an overwhelming peace and sense of strength. I knew at that time that only the strength of Christ can get us through the day.

Something else that happened beyond a complete submission and surrender was the emergence of a steadfast mind and a sound mind that is able to be renewed daily. **Isaiah 26:3-4** says, "…the steadfast of mind You will keep in perfect peace, because he trusts in you. Trust in the Lord forever, for in God the Lord, we have an everlasting rock." We continue to have strength through trust, peace, steadfastness, and soundness. We are able to have this by continuously seeking the Lord. **1 Chronicles 16:11** tells us, "…seek the Lord and his strength; seek his presence continually."

When we completely and totally submit to the Lord, we will see and experience how joy, the renewing of the mind, peace, and trust give us strength, but we will also see how Jesus gives a spirit of power and strength. **Psalm 138:3** says, "On the day I called, You answered me; You made me bold with strength in my soul."

We can call on the Lord anytime to help fight our battles. In order to do this, we need to set all our ways and our plans before the Lord. This helps us to walk in the spirit of strength and power He gives us. **Psalm 16:8** says, "I have set the Lord continually before me; because He is at my right hand, I will not be shaken." Again, we see that it is not our own strength but the strength that comes from Jesus as we trust in Him alone. This strength doesn't allow us to be timid, but allows us to be bold and courageous. **2 Timothy 1:7 states,** "For God has not given us a spirit of timidity, but of power and love and discipline."

Knowing our strength in Jesus requires self-discipline and self-control; these are two key character and behavioral traits that allow us to operate in this power. As we develop self-discipline and self-control, we can clearly see the strength and power of Jesus, which is always worthy of praise. As for myself, who once tried to operate in his own strength, I can tell you there was more defeat than victory. This leads to depression, defeat, anger, and many other terrible things.

The struggle of learning self-discipline and self-control was not fun, but it was the tool used to prune the tree so that it may produce fruit. The lessons we learn that have pain behind them are never in vain when we allow the love of Christ to penetrate our hearts. These lessons only draw us closer to the Lord.

LESSON 6

Memory Verse:
Try your best to memorize the Biblical verse. It is ok to struggle with this as memorization can be difficult. Be sure to extend grace towards one another in memorizing Bible verses. This is to help create consistency and develop a good habit of thinking about Scripture throughout the day.

> ***2 Timothy 1:7:*** *"For God has not given us a spirit of timidity, but of power and love and discipline" (Holy Bible, NASB, 2021).*

Quiet Times:
Personal time of devotion and dedication, spending time in the Scriptures with the Lord.
Psalm 112: 1, 7-8 (Monday – Wednesday)
Psalm 62: 1-2 (Thursday – Saturday)
Philippians 4:12-13 (Monday – Wednesday)
Hebrews 4: 12-16 (Thursday – Saturday)

During you quiet times follow these guidelines and write them in a journal or notebook so that you will be able to share your quiet time with your group. Share at least one quiet time with your group. Before sharing a

quiet time, please begin by having one of your brothers pray over the group.

Quiet Time – Guideline:

- Be specific in your answers, writing a paragraph for each answer.
- Key point or theme of the passage/verse – What is the author's intent to the original audience?
- Key Words – Repeated words in the text
- Emphasize word - Use a concordance or Bible dictionary to find what the context of the word means in your key verse.
- How will the application of the biblical principle make a difference in your daily walk with the Lord?
- Rewrite your key verse to make it personal to our modern time, without reading yourself into the text.
- How will this verse help you approach a lost person and tell them about the love of Jesus?
- What is the original intent of the author to the original audience?
- Is there a biblical principle from the original audience we can apply in our modern time?

- What are the differences and similarities between the original audience and our modern audience?

Lesson 6 Discussion Questions:

Be ready to share with your group how your answers and how these questions apply to a character change, and deepen your trust and faith knowing your strength comes from the Lord.

1. Has there been a specific situation when you knew that you needed to seek the Lord for strength, yet you tried to operate in your own strength? What was the outcome and how did this affect you? Is there anything you would have done differently?
2. Has there ever been a time when Jesus showed His strength in your daily walk? Was this evidence of His Word in Scripture? Did you check the evidence with Scripture to make sure you were not deceived?
3. How will walking in the strength and power Jesus gives us help your witness to both believers and non- believers? What will the result be? How will you take action trusting the strength of Jesus?
4. How has not walking in the strength of Jesus affected your faith and trust in the Word? If negatively, has this kept you from being in the

Word daily? What will you do to get back in the Word daily and have accountability amongst your brothers?

5. How will the strength of Jesus that has been given to you help build and encourage your brothers in their daily walk? How will this build your faith?

6. What happens if we do not have self-control or self-discipline? Have you made sure that you are in complete and total submission to the Lord?

Before departing for the day, have one person close out in prayer. Be sure to have an action plan for this coming week for reaching out to your brothers. Be in prayer for one another throughout the week in your growth and in deepening your relationship with our Lord and Savior Jesus Christ.

Exercise Plan – Week 9 and Week 10

Monday - chest
- Bench press (4-5 sets, 15, 12, 10, 8 reps)
- Incline bench press (4-5 sets, 15, 12, 10, 8 reps)
- Dumbbell press (4-5 sets, 15, 12, 10, 8 reps)
- Dumbbell flyes (4-5 sets, 15, 12, 10, 8 reps)
- Cable cross (4-5 sets, 15, 12, 10, 8 reps)
- Chest press (4-5 sets, 15, 12, 10, 8 reps)
- Dips (4-5 sets, 15, 12, 10, 8 reps)
- 20 minutes cardio – seated row, jog, run, elliptical, bike riding

Tuesday – back and abs
- Deadlift (4-5 sets, 15, 12, 10, 8 reps)
- Lat pulldown (4-5 sets, 15, 12, 10, 8 reps)
- Lat half-moon (4-5 sets, 15, 12, 10, 8 reps)
- Machine rows (4-5 sets, 15, 12, 10, 8 reps)
- Dumbbell rows (4-5 sets, 15, 12, 10, 8 reps)
- Weighted crunches (4-5 sets, 15, 12, 10, 8 reps)
- Leg raises (4-5 sets, 15, 12, 10, 8 reps)
- Sit-ups (4-5 sets, 15, 12, 10, 8 reps)
- 20 minutes cardio – seated row, jog, run, elliptical, bike riding

Wednesday – shoulders and traps

- Front to back military press (4-5 sets, 15, 12, 10, 8 reps)
- Arnold press (4-5 sets, 15, 12, 10, 8 reps)
- Front raises (4-5 sets, 15, 12, 10, 8 reps)
- Lateral raises (4-5 sets, 15, 12, 10, 8 reps)
- Shrugs (4-5 sets, 15, 12, 10, 8 reps)
- Delt flyes (4-5 sets, 15, 12, 10, 8 reps)
- Rear delt raises (4-5 sets, 15, 12, 10, 8 reps)
- 20 minutes cardio – seated row, jog, run, elliptical, bike riding

Thursday – arms

- Bicep curls (4-5 sets, 15, 12, 10, 8 reps)
- Barbell curls (4-5 sets, 15, 12, 10, 8 reps)
- Preacher curls (4-5 sets, 15, 12, 10, 8 reps)
- Hammer curls (4-5 sets, 15, 12, 10, 8 reps)
- Triceps pushdown (4-5 sets, 15, 12, 10, 8 reps)
- Triceps dips (4-5 sets, 15, 12, 10, 8 reps)
- Skull crusher (4-5 sets, 15, 12, 10, 8 reps)
- Triceps extension (4-5 sets, 15, 12, 10, 8 reps)
- Dumbbell kickbacks (4-5 sets, 15, 12, 10, 8 reps)
- 20 minutes cardio – seated row, jog, run, elliptical, bike riding

Friday – legs

- Squats (4-5 sets, 15, 12, 10, 8 reps)
- Leg press (4-5 sets, 15, 12, 10, 8 reps)
- Leg extension (4-5 sets, 15, 12, 10, 8 reps)
- Leg curls (4-5 sets, 15, 12, 10, 8 reps)
- Stiff-leg deadlift (4-5 sets, 15, 12, 10, 8 reps)
- Lunges (4-5 sets, 15, 12, 10, 8 reps)
- Sitting Calf raises (4-5 sets, 15, 12, 10, 8 reps)
- Standing calf raises (4-5 sets, 15, 12, 10, 8 reps)
- Donkey calf raises (4-5 sets, 15, 12, 10, 8 reps)
- 20 minutes cardio – seated row, jog, run, elliptical, bike riding

Saturday and Sunday – Recovery

As you rest and recover, be sure your family is always a priority. Your family also comes before the regular exercise routine during the week. It is far more important and valuable that you are spiritually leading your family than spending countless hours at the gym or exercising in your home gym. The exercise routine is to help you see measurable results as you go through the study each week. Be intentional with your family and help develop, build, and grow them spiritually, getting to Jesus in a deeper way.

7

PRAYING FOR OTHERS AND QUIET TIMES

What is the reason for quiet time and how does it affect us in our spiritual growth? Quiet Time is a key to the believer's success in developing a deeper relationship with the Lord. Not only does it build a deeper relationship, but it also helps us understand the spiritual side of our daily walk.

So often we get pulled into only studying the Word that we forget the spiritual aspect of our faith. When we side track into only the study of the Word it can easily become an idol the leads us into the false doctrine of intellectual religion. This idolatry leaves no room for the Holy Spirit to operate through us with the gifts that have been given to us.

One may ask, "What do you mean by 'false doctrine of intellectual religion'?" Clearly, the answer is searching out another theologian's answers before accepting the Word of God as Truth. Some people can get so deep into searching for answers that they over complicate the Word and Truth of God. Even though there are many things in Scripture that we may not understand, there is a reason for that. God will reveal what He means if we ask, have patience, and trust in His timing.

One of the biggest problems today is that people need instant gratification. and this makes it so easy and tempting to try and open the doors ourselves, thus not allowing God to open or even close doors for us. All this does is create hurt, disappointment, and a falling away from faith. So how do we face this spiritual battle head-on, and not play the victim looking for other people's sympathy which can bring instant gratification?

We need to have quiet times daily—as many as God calls you to have. In our quiet time is where we find God speaking to us through His Word and then us speaking to God through prayer. **1 John 5:14-15** says, "This is the confidence which we have before Him, that, if we ask anything according to His will, He hears us. And if we know that He hears us in whatever we ask, we know that we have requests which we have asked from Him." Now our prayers need to align with God's will, but some prayers tend to take on selfishness and pride. We must examine our hearts before entering into prayer so that we do pray according to His will.

In our communication with God through prayer from our quiet time we can see the will of God revealed for our lives. We have a clearer understanding of the Scripture we just read, and it helps us to meditate on that Scripture. The goals of quiet times and prayer are to keep us in communication with God at all times. **1 Timothy 2:8** reminds us, "Therefore I want the men in every place to pray, lifting up holy hands, without wrath and dissension."

Not only should we be praying in our quiet times, but at all times. Knowing this, it can create some anxiety and fear which can hinder us from being obedient in the will of God. **Philippians 4: 6-7** has the answer for this issue, stating, "Do not be anxious about anything, but in everything by prayer ad supplication with thanksgiving let your requests be made known to God. And the peace of God, which surpasses all understanding, will guard your hearts and your minds in Christ Jesus" (NIV, 2024). God gave us a remedy for this in that Scripture, where we find peace and strength.

As we grow and develop through our quiet times and prayer, we begin to start praying for other people. Our prayers shift from ourselves to them. This is important, as it gives us a spirit of humility that is needed to pray for others. If all we did was present our own requests before God, that would seem like we were playing victim to the trials and tribulations of life without having care or love for anyone else, let alone all creation. This puts us in disobedience to **James 4:3,** which says, "You ask and do not receive, because you ask with wrong motives, so that you may spend it on your pleasures." When we pray for others, we get a beautiful experience of seeing God work through that person and break down the pride and selfishness in our own hearts.

One of the biggest issues I have encountered in the church body today is that people will say, "I will pray for you," but then never do; they go on their merry way and forget about the person who needs prayer. How discouraging to the one who really needs prayer and has a real need for God to intervene in their life. This is one way that believers in the church body are pushed away from faith, the church body, and caring about their salvation. This can honestly be the cause of a wicked heart in some, and we are warned against this. **Proverbs 15:29** says, "The Lord is far from the wicked, but He hears the prayer of the righteous." If we practice righteousness, then we make sure we follow through in what we say, bringing people closer to the Lord. We also need to be in constant prayer, for this helps us follow through when we tell someone we will pray for them. **Romans 12:12** tells us "…rejoicing in hope, preserving in tribulation, devoted to prayer." Sometimes when we tell someone we will pray for them, but don't, it can cause tribulation in that person's life.

As we follow through in what we say and hold our words true, we find that our quiet times reveal more to us through Scripture and that we have a yearning to pray for other people. This is how we strengthen the church body, which has hurt so many people. If we create division by not praying for others when they ask, we quickly see the church body taken over by the enemy, leaving room for him to use confusion and many other impediments against the Body of Christ. We must stay true to our word, constantly build up the church, being encouraging, being in constant prayer, and growing in our quiet times with Our Lord.

LESSON 7

Memory Verse:

Try your best to memorize the Biblical verse. It is ok to struggle with this as memorization can be difficult. Be sure to extend grace towards one another in memorizing Bible verses. This is to help create consistency and develop a good habit of thinking about Scripture throughout the day.

> ***Matthew 7:7:*** *"Ask, and it will be given to you; seek, and you will find; knock, and it will be opened to you."*

Quiet Times:

Personal time of devotion and dedication, spending time in the Scriptures with the Lord.

Romans 12:19-20 (Monday – Wednesday)
James 4:1-6 (Thursday – Saturday)
1 Timothy 2:8 (Monday – Wednesday)
Philippians 4:6-7 (Thursday – Saturday)

During you quiet times follow these guidelines and write them in a journal or notebook so that you will be able to share your quiet time with your group. Share at least one quiet time with your group. Before sharing a

quiet time, please begin by having one of your brothers pray over the group.

Quiet Time – Guideline:

- Be specific in your answers, writing a paragraph for each answer.
- Key point or theme of the passage/verse – What is the author's intent to the original audience?
- Key Words – Repeated words in the text
- Emphasize word - Use a concordance or Bible dictionary to find what the context of the word means in your key verse.
- How will the application of the biblical principle make a difference in your daily walk with the Lord?
- Rewrite your key verse to make it personal to our modern time, without reading yourself into the text.
- How will this verse help you approach a lost person and tell them the love of Jesus?
- What is the original intent of the author to the original audience?
- Is there a biblical principle from the original audience we can apply in our modern time?
- What are the differences and similarities between the original audience and our modern audience?

Lesson 7 Discussion Questions:

Before you share your answers to this lesson's questions, take some time, be quiet, be still, and wait on the Lord. The time duration should be left to the Holy Spirit. Have one person pray for the time duration, then lead the group through the questions in this lesson.

1. Has God called you to start praying for others outside of your group? In what ways has He called you to pray? Have you seen a change in these people? If not, how will you continue to pray with expectation?

2. Has there ever been a time when you felt called to pray for someone during a worship service, but something prevented you from going and praying with that person? What is your interpretation of the obedience and disobedience of this? Was there anything legalistic that prevented you from following through on this calling? How will you take action next time?

3. Having gone through Book Two of *Developing a Disciple* up to this point, you should notice or have seen character and behavioral changes in yourself and in those individuals in your group. Besides your own knowledge, in what ways have you had confirmation of this? What character and behavioral changes

has God worked on in you? Why is this important?

4. What have you noticed about the intimacy of your quiet times? Have you drawn closer to the Lord? What struggles and attacks have you faced in order to do your quiet times? Have you been able to reach out to your brothers for spiritual support and guidance during these times?

5. During your quiet times, has God revealed a calling in your life that requires obedience and stepping out in faith? Has God revealed the things holding you back from walking in the will of God and becoming a vessel for Him to use? How will you approach your brothers for encouragement and support if you have been called to something specific?

6. During your quiet times have you tried different physical body position during prayer, such as kneeling, lying on your stomach on the floor, sitting, or standing? How does this physical body language change the way you pray during your quiet time?

7. Has any selfishness or pride every prevented you from reading the Word, praying for someone, teaching a class, getting involved in a ministry, or showing unconditional love towards a family member or friend? How were you able to discern the spiritual attack,

and how did you allow God to work in this time? What was the result of this, and how did it affect your daily walk?

8. What actions will you take to follow up and support your brothers during their quiet times and prayer for others? How will this deepen your relationship with your brothers? How does this apply to making disciples?

9. Is there anything now that you need prayer for, freedom from, guidance and direction over? What is your plan to present this request to God? How can your brother help to pray and support you?

10. Is there anything during the past week that needs repentance and forgiveness? How will you show unconditional love for someone this week, and let the light of Jesus shine through you, so someone else can partake in the water and Bread of Life?

Before departing your group, go around the room in prayer, giving thanks for one another. Your brotherly relationships are a gift from God that should always be held sacred to your heart. It is important to maintain unity. If you feel that there has been division in the group, please pray and select a couple other verses centered on unity to bring the group back to the Lord. Jesus should always be at the center of your group's focus. Nothing else is worth pursuing besides a life with

Jesus in control. You will have guidance and direction from the Lord as you grow deeper with quiet times, memorizing Scripture, and praying for others.

I will end this lesson with one last verse. This is an important verse, as it will lead you into freedom—if this becomes your prayer—so you can become the disciple that the Lord wants you to be.

The Cost of Following the Lord, Luke 14:25-27:

Now great crowds were traveling with him. So he turned and said to them: If anyone comes to me and does not hate his own father and mother, wife and children, brothers and sisters, yes, and even his own life, he cannot be my disciple. Whoever does not bear his own cross and come after me cannot be my disciple. (CSB, 2022)

I encourage a quiet time over this passage, as it is about unconditional love toward everyone, but hating the worldly life. Everyone deserves to hear the Good News of Jesus so they can have new birth and eternal life in paradise with our Lord and Savior.

Exercise Plan – Week 7 and Week 8

Monday
- DB side lateral raises - 5 set x 12, 10, 10, 10, 8/16, 8/16
- Barbell squat – 5 set x 12, 10, 10, 10, 8/16, 8/16
- Leg extensions – 5 set x 12, 10, 10, 10, 8/16, 8/16
- Leg curls – 5 set x 12, 10, 10, 10, 8/16, 8/16
- 20 minutes of cardio – seated row, jog, run, elliptical, bike riding, swimming

Tuesday
- Seated DB presses - 4 x 12, 12, 10, 8/16
- Seated bent over rear delt raises - 4 x 12, 12, 10/20, 10/20
- Cable side raises - 4 x 12, 12, 10, 10 Cable in front of the body or behind.
- DB front raises - 4 x 12, 12, 10, 10/10/10 Last set is a drop set. Decrease the weight each time by 5-10lbs and continue to get 10 reps until you can no longer get 10 reps.
- Shrugs with DB - 6-8 sets x Failure (use a weight that is within 80-85% of your max rep)
- 20 minutes cardio – seated row, jog, run, elliptical, bike riding, swimming

Wednesday

- Bent-over dumbbell row – 4 x 12, 12, 10, 8/16
- One-arm dumbbell row - 4 x 12, 12, 10, 8/16
- Wide-grip lat pulldown - 4 x 12, 12, 10, 8/16
- Standing dumbbell triceps extension – 4 x 12, 12, 10, 8/16
- 20 minutes cardio – seated row, jog, run, elliptical, bike riding, swimming

Thursday – Sunday

This time is intentionally reserved for family time. Do something active with your family like going for a walk, biking on trails, playing outdoor games in the back yard. This time should be an enjoyable fulfillment to your heart to recognize the gift God has given you with your family.

8

READING THE BIBLE TO UNDERSTAND

There are a lot of great Bible study tools available to us today that we can find online and in books; even some Bibles have reading plans. All of these are great tools and resources to use to supplement your time in the Word. This study you are engaged in now is a good supplement to your normal reading and spending time with the Lord. Where we need to be careful is making sure the tools and resources don't replace the time we spend with God in the Word. If they do, the reality is that you may need to hold off on the supplemental resources and pray about it. If this study were to take more time away from you being in the Word, then I would ask that you set this aside and focus on your relationship with the Lord. It is important that we spend as much time as possible in the Word; it's the only way we can renew our minds daily.

It is not only to renew our minds with reading the Word daily, and have understanding, but we need to read in order to grow spiritually. Growing spiritually will give us the understanding we crave and search for. **1 Peter 2:2** says, "Like newborn infants, long for the pure spiritual milk, that by it you may grow up into salvation" (ESV, 2024). Reading the Word to have understanding gives us a better grasp on what our salvation is, making it sacred in our hearts. If we slow down our reading, instead of trying to get 10 chapters in at a time, we can really dig deep into the meat of the scriptures and have guidance when we slow down. **Psalm 119:18** tells us, "Open my eyes, that I may behold wondrous things out of your law" (ESV, 2024). And **Psalm 119:105** reminds us, "Your word is a lamp to my feet and a light to my path" (ESV, 2024). Just in the book of Psalms in these two verses, we see that if we slow down we can have an understanding of how the scriptures will guide us and direct us.

Too many times we read too quickly and miss so much depth, which leads us to hearing only the things we want to hear. This has to be avoided, otherwise we can easily make the Bible relevant only to our feelings, which becomes a false doctrine. To avoid this, we have to slow down, use discernment, be able to be corrected, and make ourselves able to be trained in righteousness. **2 Timothy 3: 16-17** states, "All scripture is breathed out by God and is profitable for teaching, for reproof, for correcting, and for training in righteousness, that the man of God may be competent, equipped for every good work" (ESV, 2024). You can see why slowing down your reading will be fruitful in every way, as Paul told Timothy.

One of the things that happens when we slow down and read to understand the Word, is that we begin to devote our entire heart to what we are reading. We want to soak up any and all information we can; this way we can share the good news with others. Too many times, we read too fast and what we read only becomes head knowledge that stays in the head and never penetrates the heart.

We need to have the Word stored up in our hearts so we do not sin against God and don't wander from His commandments. **Psalm 119:10-11** says, "With my whole heart I seek you; let me not wander from your commandments! I have stored up your word in my heart, that I might not sin against you" (ESV, 2024). This seems like a command that if we read and partake in the Bread of Life, it must always be stored up in our hearts, otherwise we chance getting off track from our walk. This could also lead us down a path of sinning and purging, sinning and purging, which is a result of not having the Word stored up in our hearts.

In too many instances, if we only allow the Word to get in our mind, we find this is where the foolish arguments on theology, application, who's right and who's wrong come in, only leading to discouragement in the church body. We should never bring discouragement amongst our brothers and sisters; rather we should be the light we are called to be and encourage one another to bring their brothers and sister, church body, and lost souls closer to Christ.

So what is the remedy for this? How do we truly read the Word to understand so we can follow in Jesus' ways and walk in the will of God? We have to begin by a complete and total surrender to God in every area of our life. This may not be fun by any means, but as we grow and have greater understanding of the Word, the Word will fill all the empty spaces we have. **Romans 8:7** says, "For the mind that is set on the flesh is hostile to God, for it does not submit to God's law; indeed, it cannot" (ESV, 2024). We find our warning in Romans 8:7 about what happens if we don't come into complete submission. Based on however much we read the Word, we will still lack understanding.

As we find ourselves in complete and total submission, now we find ourselves obeying God and teaching sound doctrine. There are two verses that explain this to us. **Acts 5:29** says, "…but Peter and the Apostles answered, 'We must obey God rather than man.'" and **Titus 2:1** tells us, "But as for you, teach what accords with sound doctrine" (ESV, 2024).

In a current Bible study I have sat through, it is easy to see that the reading to understand Scripture has been a result of fast-paced reading. In some cases, the doctrine that is taught can be twisted and/or distorted to reflect the emotions of the person teaching at that moment. I can tell you that when this happens it almost seems that the person teaching is no longer living in their freedom, but rather taking on the appearance of

DEVELOPING A DISCIPLE

a slave spiritually. The verifying statement that is always made from the group is, "We are sinners saved by grace," which is true, but at what point will that statement change to "I am a child of God"? If reading the Word incorporated slowing down and understanding what God wants to tells us was happening, then we would see that change in the group. When we continually tell ourselves we are sinners, that leaves us looking in the rearview mirror, unable to look forward to see what is ahead.

Slowing down and reading to understand does take some self-discipline and self-control, especially for speed readers. It's not an easy task; usually when we slow down we end up having more conviction over things or situations we face daily in our lives. Conviction is an okay thing. It helps us build and grow, and have the character and behavioral change needed to soak up all we can from the Word of God.

~*~

Lesson 8

Memory verse:

Try your best to memorize the Biblical verse. It is ok to struggle with this as memorization can be difficult. Be sure to extend grace towards one another in memorizing Bible verses. This is to help create consistency and develop a good habit of thinking about Scripture throughout the day.

> *1 Peter 2:2* : "*...like newborn infants, long for the pure spiritual milk, that by it you may grow up into salvation*" *(ESV, 2024).*

Quiet Times:

Personal time of devotion and dedication, spending time in the Scriptures with the Lord.
1 Peter 2: 2- 5 (Monday – Wednesday)
Psalm 119: 9- 24 (Thursday – Saturday)
James 4: 7- 12 (Monday – Wednesday)
Romans 8: 5 – 11 (Thursday – Saturday)

During you quiet times follow these guidelines and write them in a journal or notebook so that you will be able to share your quiet time with your group. Share at least one quiet time with your group. Before sharing a

quiet time, please begin by having one of your brothers pray over the group.

Quiet Time – Guideline:

- Be specific in your answers, writing a paragraph for each answer.
- Key point or theme of the passage/verse – what is the author's intent to the original audience?
- Key Words – repeated words in the text
- Emphasize word - Use a concordance or Bible dictionary to find what the context of the word means in your key verse.
- How will the application of the biblical principle make a difference in your daily walk with the Lord?
- Rewrite your key verse to make it personal to our modern time, without reading yourself into the text.
- How will this verse help you approach a lost person and tell them the love of Jesus?
- What is the original intent of the author to the original audience?
- Is there a biblical principle from the original audience we can apply in our modern time?
- What are the differences and similarities between the original audience and our modern audience?

Lesson 8 Discussion Questions:

Before you begin sharing your questions, come together in prayer asking the Lord to guide and direct you discussion that it may be fruitful and honoring to God.

1. Can you state a time when you felt rushed through Scripture and felt like you didn't get anything out of the verses you just read? How many verses was that? Did you go back and read again? Were there any tools you used to clarify your understanding of the Scripture that you just read?

2. When you sit down to study the Word of God, is it for pleasure, or is it to know who God is and why you want to know more about Him? What difference would this make in your daily walk with God?

3. What happens when we slow down to read so that we are able to understand the Scriptures? Has God revealed anything to you when you slow down versus speed reading through His word? When was the last time you sped read through the scriptures? How will you correct this behavior?

4. What is the effect of a hostile mind and how does that influence people around you in church, work, home, and with friends? What do

you do when a hostile mind comes against you? How are you able to get your mind focused back on God and His Word?

5. How will reading to understand help you with teaching the Word of God to others in the church body? Have you ever been asked to teach a class, Sunday school, preach, or lead worship? If yes, what difference will this make in having a truth-filled doctrine? If no, how will you use the understanding of the Word to help build the church body?

6. What is your first step if you read a verse and don't understand what it means? Why are you seeking clarity of this verse? Will the clarity bring you closer to God or legalism? How will this help your daily walk and being in the word daily?

7. Write a short paragraph on how you exercised self-control and self-discipline to slow down reading the Word and soak up everything God wanted to reveal to you. This only needs to be 5 – 7 sentences long.

Lesson 8 Challenge

This week as you read outside your quiet times, challenge yourself to really dive in deep with Scripture. Slow yourself down, think and meditate on every word you read. Let the Word penetrate your heart.

Before departing this week, go around the group praying for one another and over the group as a whole. Remember to follow up with your brothers this week and see if you can help clarify any questions they may have through their reading or quiet times. Be humble in your approach to help clarify any questions your brothers have. This means to be gentle and listen with the intent to understand where your brothers are at. It is not easy to be open and honest in a group setting, and it takes much courage. If a clarification question is needed, ask a clarification question to understand, not to judge. Encourage one another, and always build your brothers up.

Exercise Plan – Week 7 and Week 8

Monday

- DB side Lateral Raises - 5 set x 12,10,10,10,8/16, 8/16
- Barbell Squat – 5 set x 12, 10, 10, 10, 8/16, 8/16
- Leg Extensions – 5 set x 12, 10, 10, 10, 8/16, 8/16
- Leg Curls – 5 set x 12, 10, 10, 10, 8/16, 8/16
- 20 minutes of cardio – seated row, jog, run, elliptical, bike riding, swimming

Tuesday

- Seated DB Presses - 4 x 12,12,10,8/16
- Seated Bent Over Rear Delt Raises - 4 x 12, 12, 10/20, 10/20
- Cable Side Raises - 4 x 12,12,10,10 Cable in front of the body or behind.
- DB Front Raises - 4 x 12,12,10, 10/10/10 Last set is a drop set. Decrease the weight each time by 5-10lbs and continue to get 10 reps until you can no longer get 10 reps.
- Shrugs with DB - 6-8 sets x Failure (use a weight that is within 80-85% of your max rep)
- 20 minutes cardio – seated row, jog, run, elliptical, bike riding, swimming

Wednesday

- Bent-over dumbbell row - 4 x 12,12,10,8/16
- One-arm dumbbell row – 4 x 12,12,10,8/16
- Wide-grip lat pulldown - 4 x 12,12,10,8/16
- Standing dumbbell triceps extension -4 x 12,12,10,8/16
- 20 minutes cardio – seated row, jog, run, elliptical, bike riding, swimming

Thursday – Sunday

This time is intentionally reserved for family time. Do something active with your family like going for a walk, biking on trails, playing outdoor games in the back yard. This time should be an enjoyable fulfillment to your heart, to recognize the gift God has given you with your family.

9

BUILDING PATIENCE

Patience is one of the key areas for a believer. Not only is it required of us as believers, but it also helps develop our character. We see patience all over the Old and New Testament, and for good reason. If we did not have patience, then how could we proclaim the Truth of the Gospel with love? **Romans 8:25** gives us a prime example of patience, stating "but if we hope for what we do not see, we wait for it with patience" (ESV, 2024). Patience helps us with clarity and understanding, not only when it comes to sharing the good new but also when we partake in the Bread of Life deepening our relationship with our Savior Jesus Christ.

I have seen so many times where patience has started out with good intentions but never reaches its full potential, causing anger, irritability, frustration, defeat, depression and so on. We do have a deep and very clear warning of the implications of not exercising patience. **Ecclesiastes 7:9** tells us, "Do not be eager in your heart to be angry, for anger resides in the bosom of fools." That is a pretty clear statement on not allowing patience in our daily walk. This is one way the enemy shoots his flaming arrows at us to keep us from operating in the gifts from the Holy Spirit. **Proverbs 15:18** states that "a hot-tempered man stirs up strife, but the slow to anger calms a dispute."

We have to think about what patience produces in our daily walk as Christians. What we are discussing here is only the surface level of what patience really is. The main theme for us is about a character change, leaving the old ways and becoming a new creation in Christ. For this we need endurance, encouragement, accountability, and the Truth of the Living Word of God. **Romans 5:4** says, "…and endurance produces character, and character produces hope" (ESV, 2024). **Hebrews 10:36** states, "For you have need of endurance, so that when you have done the will of God you may receive what is promised" (ESV, 2024). **James 5:7-8** tells us to "…be patient, therefore, brothers, until the coming of the Lord. See how the farmer waits for the precious fruit of the earth. Being patient about it, until it receives the early and the late rains. You also, be patient. Establish your hearts, for the coming of the Lord is at hand" (ESV, 2024).

We can see how important patience really is. When we look at David, we can see an example of patience. If David never exercised his patience, then how would he have ever heard from the Lord? David need patience in order to hear clearly for direction and guidance, even to kneel before the Lord in repentance. **Psalm 40:1** says, "I waited patiently for the Lord; He inclined to me and heard my cry."

Now if David had not shown patience, he could easily have been distracted, manipulated, or even worse had a subversion of his faith. Patience helped build and develop David's character and led him into repentance.

As we endure our daily walk we should always have patience set upon our hearts. We never know when the Lord will give us a chance to lead them to the cross. With patience we can bring a clear understanding to what the Truth of the Gospel is and we also get to display the Love of Jesus.

Another point I would like to touch on with patience is that we find strength and power that is a direct result of patience. **Colossians 1:11** says, "…being strengthened with all power, according to His glorious might, so that you may have great endurance and patience, joyfully" (CSB, 2022). **Romans 5:3-4** says, "…and not only that, but we also rejoice in our sufferings, knowing that suffering produces endurance, and endurance produces character, and character produces hope" (ESV, 2024).

After knowing that in hard times in our walk, if we just remain patient, we will have joy, hope, peace, clarity, a reason to rejoice. We know that this hope will not fail us, and as **Romans 5:5** continues, "…and hope does not disappoint, because the love of God has been poured out within our hearts through the Holy Spirit who was given to us." With patience in our daily walk, we can be assured that God's Love has covered us. We are able to withstand the attack of the enemy, resist the devil, and remove ourselves from temptation.

So many times you see a believer who is excited and ready to hit the streets and proclaim the Good News. I think that this zeal is a good thing and needed for all believers, however, this can also be an open door for the attack of the enemy if not treated carefully and with patience. An excited believer, or newly born again believer, is one of the greatest enjoyments to be around. Their heart is on fire and they are ready to live for Christ at any cost. They have experienced the freedom and know the freedom they have in our Lord. This is so encouraging for others to be around. But one thing we must teach, display, and live is patience.

Patience is key to our growth, our relationship with the Lord, having knowledge and wisdom of the Word, and developing a character that is required to walk daily in the Word of God. Be Patient. Be Kind. Wait upon the Lord. **Psalm 27:14** says, "Wait for the Lord; be strong and let your heart take courage; Yes, wait for the Lord!"

Before we go into our lesson, be quiet and still before the Lord. Listen for him to speak to you. So many times believers feel called into full time ministry, career change, missions, volunteering, yet we need to be patient and wait on the Lord to give us guidance. Otherwise we chance chasing our emotions rather than the will of God.

LESSON 9

Memory Verse:
Try your best to memorize the Biblical verse. It is ok to struggle with this as memorization can be difficult. Be sure to extend grace towards one another in memorizing Bible verses. This is to help create consistency and develop a good habit of thinking about Scripture throughout the day.

> ***Psalm 27:14:*** *"Wait for the Lord; be strong and let your heart take courage; Yes, wait for the Lord!"*

Quiet Times:
Personal time of devotion and dedication, spending time in the Scriptures with the Lord.
Luke 21: 14-19 (Monday – Wednesday)
Proverbs 14: 29-35 (Thursday – Saturday)
James 5: 7-11 (Monday – Wednesday)
2 Timothy 4: 1-3 (Thursday – Saturday)

During your quiet times follow these guidelines and write them in a journal or notebook so that you will be able to share your quiet time with your group. Share at least one quiet time with your group. Before sharing a

quiet time, please begin by having one of your brothers pray over the group.

Quiet Time – Guideline:

- Be specific in your answers, writing a paragraph for each answer.
- Key point or theme of the passage/verse – What is the author's intent to the original audience?
- Key Words – Repeated words in the text
- Emphasize word - Use a concordance or Bible dictionary to find what the context of the word means in your key verse.
- How will the application of the biblical principle make a difference in your daily walk with the Lord?
- Rewrite your key verse to make it personal to our modern time, without reading yourself into the text.
- How will this verse help you approach a lost person and tell them the love of Jesus?
- What is the original intent of the author to the original audience?
- Is there a biblical principle from the original audience we can apply in our modern time?
- What are the differences and similarities between the original audience and our modern audience?

Lesson 9 Discussion Question:

Before you begin sharing your questions, come together in prayer asking the Lord to guide and direct you discussion that it may be fruitful and honoring to God.

1. Knowing how important patience is to our daily walk, how have you exercised patience this week? What are implications of not practicing patience, how would this affect you in your Christian walk?
2. When was the last time you allowed anger, irritation, and frustration to come in front of patience? Did this allow a past sin, vice, stronghold or struggle to come back into your life?
3. How will patience help you in repentance and forgiveness of others, and in allowing the Holy Spirit to purify your heart and mind so you can walk in the will of God? Why is this important to you and your relationship with our Heavenly Father?
4. Are you ready now to allow patience be a part of your daily walk so that you may have a true witness of the Gospel of Truth? What steps and actions will you apply to practice patience daily? Will you need accountability?

5. With the brothers with whom you study, has there ever been a time that patience was pushed aside to either prove a point, or bring your beliefs before your brothers? How did this affect your relationship? Was there time for repentance and forgiveness? If not, will you seek and search repentance and forgiveness?

6. With patience, what can you do to help encourage, build and sharpen your brothers? What results will this have in your brotherly relationships? How will this model a truthful witness to the church body you serve, and why is this witness important to the church body?

7. When was the last time you were impatient with yourself during your memory verses? What caused you to be impatient? What actions can you and your brothers take to help provide and build patience so you long to memorize scripture?

8. Are you willing and ready to allow patience to be part of your growth? Are you understanding and ready for the hard times, trials, and challenges that come with developing patience? Will you turn the other cheek or attack the situation? Why is this important to you? What will happen to your character if you allow patience to be a part of your life?

DEVELOPING A DISCIPLE

As you converse about the questions from Lesson 9, please remember to practice patience with your brothers. With patience, we are able to listen with understanding. We have a clearer understand or how and where we can help support each other and the church body. Please remain in prayer for your brothers this week, as practicing patience can reveal hidden things of the heart. Be kind and show love towards one another.

Before departing this week from your group, have the leader pray over the group. Pray for guidance and protection as you set out to practice patience. Be understanding, slow to speak, quick to listen, and show love and kindness for one another. This lesson is especially important for those of you with a family, wife, and kids. Patience will help develop a loving atmosphere for your entire family as they see you transform into the Warrior and Man of God that God designed you to be. Please ask your family to be in prayer for you as well.

Exercise Plan – Week 3 and Week 4

Monday - chest
- Bench Press (4-5 sets, 15, 12, 10, 8 reps)
- Incline bench press (4-5 sets, 15, 12, 10, 8 reps)
- Dumbbell flyes (4-5 sets, 15, 12, 10, 8 reps)
- Cable cross (4-5 sets, 15, 12, 10, 8 reps)
- Chest press (4-5 sets, 15, 12, 10, 8 reps)
- Dips (4-5 sets, 15, 12, 10, 8 reps)
- 20 minutes cardio – seated row, jog, run, elliptical, bike riding

Tuesday – back and abs
- Deadlift (4-5 sets, 15, 12, 10, 8 reps)
- Lat pulldown (4-5 sets, 15, 12, 10, 8 reps)
- Lat half-moon (4-5 sets, 15, 12, 10, 8 reps)
- Machine rows (4-5 sets, 15, 12, 10, 8 reps)
- Dumbbell rows (4-5 sets, 15, 12, 10, 8 reps)
- Weighted crunches (4-5 sets, 15, 12, 10, 8 reps)
- 20 minutes cardio – seated row, jog, run, elliptical, bike riding

Wednesday – shoulders and traps
- Front to back military press (4-5 sets, 15, 12, 10, 8 reps)
- Front raises (4-5 sets, 15, 12, 10, 8 reps)

- Lateral raises (4-5 sets, 15, 12, 10, 8 reps)
- Shrugs (4-5 sets, 15, 12, 10, 8 reps)
- Delt flyes (4-5 sets, 15, 12, 10, 8 reps)
- Rear delt raises (4-5 sets, 15, 12, 10, 8 reps)
- 20 minutes cardio – seated row, jog, run, elliptical, bike riding

Thursday – arms

- Bicep curls (4-5 sets, 15, 12, 10, 8 reps)
- Barbell curls (4-5 sets, 15, 12, 10, 8 reps)
- Preacher curls (4-5 sets, 15, 12, 10, 8 reps)
- Hammer curls (4-5 sets, 15, 12, 10, 8 reps)
- Triceps pushdown (4-5 sets, 15, 12, 10, 8 reps)
- Skull crusher (4-5 sets, 15, 12, 10, 8 reps)
- Triceps extension (4-5 sets, 15, 12, 10, 8 reps)
- Dumbbell kickbacks (4-5 sets, 15, 12, 10, 8 reps)
- 20 minutes cardio – seated row, jog, run, elliptical, bike riding

Friday – legs

- Squats (4-5 sets, 15, 12, 10, 8 reps)
- Leg press (4-5 sets, 15, 12, 10, 8 reps)
- Leg extension (4-5 sets, 15, 12, 10, 8 reps)
- Leg curls (4-5 sets, 15, 12, 10, 8 reps)
- Stiff-leg deadlift (4-5 sets, 15, 12, 10, 8 reps)
- Lunges (4-5 sets, 15, 12, 10, 8 reps)

- Sitting calf raises (4-5 sets, 15, 12, 10, 8 reps)
- 20 minutes cardio – seated row, jog, run, elliptical, bike riding

Saturday and Sunday – Recovery

As you rest and recover, be sure your family is always a priority. Your family also comes before the regular exercise routine during the week. It is far more important and valuable that you are spiritually leading your family than spending countless hours at the gym or exercising in your home gym. The exercise routine is to help you see measurable results as you go through the study each week. Be intentional with your family and help develop, build, and grow them spiritually getting to Jesus in a deeper way.

10

Having the Mind of Christ

Having the mind of Christ is something that completely transforms the believer. Now we understand that in order to have a mind like Christ, we have a solid foundation in the Word of God and a relationship built upon the solid rock. Not only is this transforming, but it also challenges us to have a different perspective on life and also how we view the people around us. The closer we get to having a Christ-like mind, the more we see the spiritual battle around us. Jesus will also reveal more to us through His Word.

So how do we prepare ourselves to have a Christ like mind? We turn to **Romans 12: 2** and get one of the first ways we are able to transform our minds into having a mind that is centered on Christ and His Word. **Romans 12:2** says, "Do not be conformed to this world, but be transformed by the renewal of your mind, that by testing you may discern what is the will of God, what is good and acceptable and perfect" (ESV, 2024). As heavy and deep as that verse is, we need to renew our minds daily in the Word. The renewing of the mind through the Word helps us to break free from the impure, negative, impulsive thoughts that enslave us to darkness.

If our mind is always enslaved, how are we able to allow the Word of God to penetrate our hearts? As our minds become more like Christ, our hearts are now in acceptance of the Word of God, allowing springs of life to flow from the heart. **Proverbs 4:23** tells us to "…keep your heart with all vigilance, for from it flow the springs of life" (ESV, 2024). We see now that the heart and mind are connected; this is why having a Christ-like mind is of great importance. In no way is this an easy task for any of us who are still living here on earth! There are always going to be challenges that are ahead of us that will challenge our mindset, attitude, and character. The one thing we need to remember is that if we don't have a Christ-like mind, we can quickly be deceived, leading to an unstable and chaotic mind. **James 1:8** says, "He is a double-minded man, unstable in all his ways" (ESV, 2024).

We strive to have a Christ like mind so we bring consistency, continuity, clarity, conviction, and calmness to our daily walk. With these characteristics we find ourselves able to consume the word of God and retain what we have learned, or what God has revealed to us in His Word. **Jeremiah 33:3** even gives us a hint at how a Christ- like mind will not only benefit us but others as well. **Jeremiah 33:3** says, "Call to me and I will answer you, and will tell you great and hidden things that you have not known" (ESV, 2024).

Great and hidden things not known can only be revealed by God Himself if we submit ourselves to having a Christ-like mind. Not only that, but having a Christ- like mind also helps up deepen our trust and faith in the Word of God. We have a promise we can cling to if our minds are pure and trusting of God in faith. **Matthew 21:22** says, "…and whatever you ask in prayer, you will receive, if you have faith" (ESV, 2024). A Christ-like mind changes the way we pray, and it allows us to pray according to the will of God our Father. We know by faith we will receive whatever we ask in prayer, because the Christ-like mind wants to seek the will of God. So many times this gets twisted in ways that you see the believer praying for material gains, selfish power and entitlement, the best life now in the immediate. Prayer and Faith need to be approached with a Christ-like mind so that we truly ask for what is in the will of God which is revealed to us through His Word.

Our Heavenly Father gives us so much support in His Word why our mindset is important. It aligns our whole being with the Word of God and sets our hearts and minds on the things above, and not on the immediate, now, self-gratifying things of the world. **Colossians 3:2** tells us to "…set your minds on things that are above, not on things that are on earth" (ESV, 2024). Another support of a Christ like mind, is

Jeremiah 29:11, which states, "For I know the plans I have for you, declares the Lord, plans for welfare and not for evil, to give you a future and hope" (ESV, 2024). And again in **Matthew 7:7,** we are reminded to **"…**ask, and it will be given to you; seek, and you will find; knock, and it will be opened to you." (ESV, 2024) All of these supporting scriptures are given to us so we can walk in the will of God and seek the things of God, not to benefit us in selfish ways, but to be able to share Christ with others and fulfill the calling that God has in our lives.

If we don't have a Christ-like mind we won't have clarity, then we end up turning our faith into an emotional experience that will only leave us sad, depressed, lonely, defeated, and not wanting to run this race. There is power and Truth in the Christ-like mind. As we search the scriptures, knowing that ever word is the living, breathing, inspired Word of God, we will renew our minds daily. In the times we live in today, renewing our minds daily to have a Christ-like mind is necessary if we are to help lead the lost to Christ, build the church, and strengthen each other.

Lesson 10

Memory verse:
Try your best to memorize the Biblical verse. It is ok to struggle with this as memorization can be difficult. Be sure to extend grace towards one another in memorizing Bible verses. This is to help create consistency and develop a good habit of thinking about Scripture throughout the day.

> ***Jeremiah 29:11:*** *"For I know the plans I have for you, declares the Lord, plans for welfare and not for evil, to give you a future and a hope"* *(ESV, 2024).*

Quiet Times:
Personal time of devotion and dedication, spending time in the Scriptures with the Lord.
Matthew 7: 7-12 (Monday – Wednesday)
Colossians 3: 1-2 (Thursday – Saturday)
Proverbs 16: 1-9 (Monday – Wednesday)
Matthew 21: 21-22 (Thursday – Saturday)

During your quiet times, follow these guidelines and write them in a journal or notebook so that you will be able to share your quiet time with your group. Share at least one quiet time with your group. Before sharing a quiet time, please begin by having one of your brothers pray over the group.

Quiet Time – Guideline:

- Be specific in your answers, writing a paragraph for each answer.
- Key point or theme of the passage/verse – What is the author's intent to the original audience?
- Key Words – Repeated words in the text
- Emphasize word - Use a concordance or Bible dictionary to find what the context of the word means in your key verse.
- How will the application of the biblical principle make a difference in your daily walk with the Lord?
- Rewrite your key verse to make it personal to our modern time, without reading yourself into the text.
- How will this verse help you approach a lost person and tell them the love of Jesus?
- What is the original intent of the author to the original audience?
- Is there a biblical principle from the original audience we can apply in our modern time?

- What are the differences and similarities between the original audience and our modern audience?

Lesson 10 Discussion Questions:

Before sharing your quiet time with the group. Pray that your discussion would be fruitful and encouraging to one another. Go around the group and pray over your conversation.

1. In what ways does having a Christ-like mind help build, edify, strengthen, and encourage not only the believer, but also the church body?
2. Why is having a Christ-like mind important to you? What will this do to your daily walk with God?
3. Has there been a time in your walk when pride has overtaken your Christ-like mind? What were the ramifications? Did this lead to repentance and forgiveness, or did it keep you steered in a direction leading away from the Word of God?
4. Why is the daily renewal of your mind important not only to you as a believer, but also to the church body?
5. How does the enemy keep the mind and heart separated? What happens when we don't allow the Word to penetrate our heart with the daily renewing of our minds? Have you experienced

defeat in this area, or victory? How did that affect your witness?

6. In what ways will you help encourage, build and support your brothers with the daily renewing of their minds? List five ways that you can help your brothers develop a Christ-like mind.

7. Are you and your brothers willing and ready to hold each other accountable to having a Christ-like mind so that you may present the Word of God in Truth to others around you?

8. How will a Christ-like mind help you build disciples, keep disciples, and witness to the lost?

9. List five actions you and your brothers will take to have accountability for each other this week. Are you committed to these actions?

Before departing, pray for one another. Remember to be patient, kind and loving as you strive to develop a Christ-like mind and be the witness that God has called you to be.

Exercise Plan – Week 3 and Week 4

Monday - chest
- Bench press (4-5 sets, 15, 12, 10, 8 reps)
- Incline bench press (4-5 sets, 15, 12, 10, 8 reps)
- Dumbbell flyes (4-5 sets, 15, 12, 10, 8 reps)
- Cable cross (4-5 sets, 15, 12, 10, 8 reps)
- Chest press (4-5 sets, 15, 12, 10, 8 reps)
- Dips (4-5 sets, 15, 12, 10, 8 reps)
- 20 minutes cardio – seated row, jog, run, elliptical, bike riding

Tuesday – back and abs
- Deadlift (4-5 sets, 15, 12, 10, 8 reps)
- Lat pulldown (4-5 sets, 15, 12, 10, 8 reps)
- Lat half-moon (4-5 sets, 15, 12, 10, 8 reps)
- Machine rows (4-5 sets, 15, 12, 10, 8 reps)
- Dumbbell rows (4-5 sets, 15, 12, 10, 8 reps)
- Weighted crunches (4-5 sets, 15, 12, 10, 8 reps)
- 20 minutes cardio – seated row, jog, run, elliptical, bike riding

Wednesday – shoulders and traps
- Front to back military press (4-5 sets, 15, 12, 10, 8 reps)
- Front raises (4-5 sets, 15, 12, 10, 8 reps)

- Lateral raises (4-5 sets, 15, 12, 10, 8 reps)
- Shrugs (4-5 sets, 15, 12, 10, 8 reps)
- Delt flyes (4-5 sets, 15, 12, 10, 8 reps)
- Rear delt raises (4-5 sets, 15, 12, 10, 8 reps)
- 20 minutes cardio – seated row, jog, run, elliptical, bike riding

Thursday – arms

- Bicep curls (4-5 sets, 15, 12, 10, 8 reps)
- Barbell curls (4-5 sets, 15, 12, 10, 8 reps)
- Preacher curls (4-5 sets, 15, 12, 10, 8 reps)
- Hammer curls (4-5 sets, 15, 12, 10, 8 reps)
- Triceps pushdown (4-5 sets, 15, 12, 10, 8 reps)
- Skull crusher (4-5 sets, 15, 12, 10, 8 reps)
- Triceps extension (4-5 sets, 15, 12, 10, 8 reps)
- Dumbbell kickbacks (4-5 sets, 15, 12, 10, 8 reps)
- 20 minutes cardio – seated row, jog, run, elliptical, bike riding

Friday – legs

- Squats (4-5 sets, 15, 12, 10, 8 reps)
- Leg press (4-5 sets, 15, 12, 10, 8 reps)
- Leg extension (4-5 sets, 15, 12, 10, 8 reps)
- Leg curls (4-5 sets, 15, 12, 10, 8 reps)
- Stiff-leg deadlift (4-5 sets, 15, 12, 10, 8 reps)
- Lunges (4-5 sets, 15, 12, 10, 8 reps)

- Sitting Calf raises (4-5 sets, 15, 12, 10, 8 reps)
- 20 minutes cardio – seated row, jog, run, elliptical, bike riding

Saturday and Sunday – Recovery

As you rest and recover, be sure that your family is always a priority. Your family also comes before the regular exercise routine during the week. It is far more important and valuable that you are spiritually leading your family than spending countless hours at the gym or exercising in your home gym. The exercise routine is to help you see measurable results as you go through the study each week. Be intentional with your family and help develop, build, and grow them spiritually getting to Jesus in a deeper way.

11

CARING FOR THE CHURCH BODY

We have a special privilege today being in the church body. We have a spiritual family, a spiritual hospital; we find encouragement, joy and peace. As believers, our church body is something we need to care for and look after. We have opportunities to help our brothers and sisters in the church in ways that the outside world cannot help. We also are able to create solid relationships built on the truth of the living and breathing Word of God. How beautiful is that! The church body is really like a family. We get the wise grandparents, the crazy and awesome kids, that funny aunt and uncle, brothers, sisters — honestly looks a lot like a family outside the church walls—so we must treat it like that in order to have unity and step away from division.

One of the best ways we can help care for the church body is to bring unity to the church. We find a prime example of unity amongst the body of the church in **1 Peter 3:8, that states,** "Finally, all of you, have unity of mind, sympathy, brotherly love, being in full accord and of one mind" (ESV, 2024). This verse reminds us about what is required to bring unity in our church today. Today's culture tends to lean heavily towards the direction of division, which only leaves us vulnerable to fall into the enemy's traps.

We find another example in **Romans 12: 4-5**, which tells us, "For just as we have many members in one body and all the members do not have the same function, so we, who are many, are one body in Christ, and individually members one of another." What a support shown through this verse how important unity is to God.

Unity in the church body leads us all to worship and lift our praises with one voice. **Romans 15: 6** says, "…so that with one accord you may with one voice glorify the God and Father of our Lord Jesus Christ." Unity really is the way we can care for our church body, and it brings us all together so we can tend to each other's needs. Where there is unity we find strength; where there is division we find defeat.

Knowing that we are all one body and that unity is what creates this amazing bond with all believers, we then look to, **1 Corinthians 12: 13** and find Paul saying, "For by one Spirit we were all baptized into one body, whether Jews or Greeks, whether slaves or free, and we were all made to drink of one Spirit." What a beautiful picture this is of how being baptized into one Spirit for the church body!

When we allow this verse to penetrate our heart we can further help and care for the church body. We must look at one more scripture in order to understand how we can care for the church body. **Ephesians 4: 16** states that "…from whom the whole body, being fitted and held together by what every joint supplies, according to the proper working of each individual part, causes the growth of the body for the building up of itself in love." Now in this verse is a key word into how we care for the church body. That key word is LOVE.

Without love, we can't truly care for the church body in any way, since without love there is darkness, and if there is darkness, there is no light. So, we must always approach caring for the church body in the Love of Christ. In Love we not only care, encourage, strengthen, and build the church body, but also we equip all members of the body of Christ to receive the fullness of Christ. **Ephesians 4: 11-13** states, "And he gave the apostles, the prophets, the evangelists, the shepherds and teachers, to equip the saints for the work of ministry, for building up the body of Christ, until we all attain to the unity of the faith and of the knowledge of the Son of God, to mature manhood, to the measure of the stature of the fullness of Christ" (ESV, 2024).

What a responsibility we have as believers, especially disciples. This is not an easy task with a great cost to it; much sacrifice is needed to truly care for the church body. This is possible according to **Ephesians 4:32** stating, "Be kind to one another, tenderhearted, forgiving one another, as God in Christ forgave you" (ESV, 2024). We can find strength in this verse seeing the Love of Christ be at the center of how we tend to the church body. **John 13:35** tells us, "By this all people will know that you are my disciples, if you have love for one another" (ESV, 2024). A church body that knows they have disciples dedicated to seeking, searching, worshiping, loving, acknowledging, and trusting in God and His living Word will see unity in the Body of Christ. The church body will be cared for at any cost. Hearts and behaviors will produce character changes, bringing the church body into the freedom they have in their salvation in Christ Jesus, Our Savior.

If we are to care for the church body today, we need to set aside all opinions, theological debates, and arguments, and let the truth of the Word of God speak to us directly. We need to always allow the Love of Christ to be at the center of everything we do and allow our Lord to guide us with his Holy Spirit. I've noticed in today's church the dynamic seems to be who can outsmart whom, and who can outperform in their works or volunteering. This is not only a trap set by the, but also it quickly causes hurt and division, no longer leaving the church body to be cared for. This is not something we must take lightly; we must allow the heaviness of this great responsibility to penetrate our hearts so we can honor Our Lord and Savior Jesus

Christ and build His church and prepare it for His second coming.

Lesson 11

Memory Verse:
Try your best to memorize the Biblical verse. It is ok to struggle with this as memorization can be difficult. Be sure to extend grace towards one another in memorizing Bible verses. This is to help create consistency and develop a good habit of thinking about Scripture throughout the day.

> *John 13:35* "*By this all people will know that you are my disciples, if you have love for one another*" *(ESV, 2024).*

Quiet Times:
Personal time of devotion and dedication, spending time in the Scriptures with the Lord.
Romans 12: 9 – 18 (Monday – Wednesday)
Romans 13: 11 – 14 (Thursday – Saturday)
Ephesians 4: 1 – 32 (Monday – Wednesday)
1 Corinthians 12: 1 – 18 (Thursday – Saturday)

During your quiet times follow these guidelines and write them in a journal or notebook so that you will be able to share your quiet time with your group. Share at least one quiet time with your group. Before sharing a quiet time, please begin by having one of your brothers pray over the group.

Quiet Time – Guideline:

- Be specific in your answers, writing a paragraph for each answer.
- Key point or theme of the passage/verse – What is the author's intent to the original audience?
- Key Words – Repeated words in the text
- Emphasize word - Use a concordance or Bible dictionary to find what the context of the word means in your key verse.
- How will the application of the biblical principle make a difference in your daily walk with the Lord?
- Rewrite your key verse to make it personal to our modern time, without reading yourself into the text.
- How will this verse help you approach a lost person and tell them about the love of Jesus?
- What is the original intent of the author to the original audience?
- Is there a biblical principle from the original audience we can apply in our modern time?

- What are the differences and similarities between the original audience and our modern audience?

Lesson 11 Discussion Questions:

Before sharing your quiet time with the group, pray that your discussion will be fruitful and encouraging to one another. Go around the group and pray over your conversation.

1. When have you been able to help care for the church body, what responsibility did God call you to? Did this responsibility draw believers closer to God and His Word, or did it push the believer further away?
2. What are your motivation and intention for helping care for the church body? Are there any selfish ambitions or motivations? In what ways will you make sure you are being guided by the Holy Spirit, and not the emotions of your own heart? Why are the emotions of the heart deceiving when one is caring for the church body? Are you ready to serve the Body of Christ in love, kindness, peace and patience?
3. Serving and caring for the Body Christ requires peace and patience. How will you display peace and patience in the Body of Christ? Is there any part of your character that will need to change in order to serve and care? By serving and

caring for the Body of Christ, what will this do in your church body?

4. Knowing that Love is a core essential in caring for the Body of Christ, has there ever been a time when pride, selfishness, anger, and irritation came before Love? What was the influence behind the behavior? Were you able to seek repentance and forgiveness? Has Love been established?

5. In what ways can you serve and care for your brothers this week, showing the Love of Christ Jesus?

6. How will you display your discipleship in the church body with the Love of Christ Jesus?

7. Is there anyone now whom God has allowed His Holy Spirit to place upon your heart and needs the Love of Jesus? How will you reach out to this person? Were they accepting of your message of the Love of Jesus? How will you continue to follow up with this person?

Before parting ways today, go around your group and pray for one another. Make a plan to follow up once with each other this week specifically on caring for the church body and how you will take action to present the Love of Christ Jesus in your church. Remember to be patient, be kind, show love, and walk in the light of our Lord Jesus Christ.

Exercise Plan – Week 3 and Week 4

Monday - chest
- Bench press (4-5 sets, 15, 12, 10, 8 reps)
- Incline bench press (4-5 sets, 15, 12, 10, 8 reps)
- Dumbbell flyes (4-5 sets, 15, 12, 10, 8 reps)
- Cable cross (4-5 sets, 15, 12, 10, 8 reps)
- Chest press (4-5 sets, 15, 12, 10, 8 reps)
- Dips (4-5 sets, 15, 12, 10, 8 reps)
- 20 minutes cardio – seated row, jog, run, elliptical, bike riding

Tuesday – back and abs
- Deadlift (4-5 sets, 15, 12, 10, 8 reps)
- Lat pulldown (4-5 sets, 15, 12, 10, 8 reps)
- Lat half-moon (4-5 sets, 15, 12, 10, 8 reps)
- Machine rows (4-5 sets, 15, 12, 10, 8 reps)
- Dumbbell rows (4-5 sets, 15, 12, 10, 8 reps)
- Weighted crunches (4-5 sets, 15, 12, 10, 8 reps)
- 20 minutes cardio – seated row, jog, run, elliptical, bike riding

Wednesday – shoulders and traps
- Front to back military press (4-5 sets, 15, 12, 10, 8 reps)
- Front raises (4-5 sets, 15, 12, 10, 8 reps)

- Lateral raises (4-5 sets, 15, 12, 10, 8 reps)
- Shrugs (4-5 sets, 15, 12, 10, 8 reps)
- Delt flyes (4-5 sets, 15, 12, 10, 8 reps)
- Rear delt raises (4-5 sets, 15, 12, 10, 8 reps)
- 20 minutes cardio – seated row, jog, run, elliptical, bike riding

Thursday – arms

- Bicep curls (4-5 sets, 15, 12, 10, 8 reps)
- Barbell curls (4-5 sets, 15, 12, 10, 8 reps)
- Preacher curls (4-5 sets, 15, 12, 10, 8 reps)
- Hammer curls (4-5 sets, 15, 12, 10, 8 reps)
- Triceps pushdown (4-5 sets, 15, 12, 10, 8 reps)
- Skull crusher (4-5 sets, 15, 12, 10, 8 reps)
- Triceps extension (4-5 sets, 15, 12, 10, 8 reps)
- Dumbbell kickbacks (4-5 sets, 15, 12, 10, 8 reps)
- 20 minutes cardio – seated row, jog, run, elliptical, bike riding

Friday – legs

- Squats (4-5 sets, 15, 12, 10, 8 reps)
- Leg press (4-5 sets, 15, 12, 10, 8 reps)
- Leg extension (4-5 sets, 15, 12, 10, 8 reps)
- Leg curls (4-5 sets, 15, 12, 10, 8 reps)
- Stiff-leg deadlift (4-5 sets, 15, 12, 10, 8 reps)
- Lunges (4-5 sets, 15, 12, 10, 8 reps)

- Sitting Calf raises (4-5 sets, 15, 12, 10, 8 reps)
- 20 minutes cardio – seated row, jog, run, elliptical, bike riding

Saturday and Sunday – Recovery

As you rest and recover, be sure that your family is always a priority. Your family also comes before the regular exercise routine during the week. It is far more important and valuable that you are spiritually leading your family than spending countless hours at the gym or exercising in your home gym. The exercise routine is to help you see measurable results as you go through the study each week. Be intentional with your family and help develop, build, and grow them spiritually getting to Jesus in a deeper way.

12

FUNDAMENTALS OF EVANGELISM

Evangelism can be a fruitful experience for the believer if performed under the guidelines of the Word of God. We see so many places in Scripture why evangelism is so important, and how we can apply it to our daily walk with God. **Mark 16: 15** says, "…and he said to them, "Go into all the world and proclaim the gospel to the whole creation" (ESV, 2024). We were told by Jesus Himself that this is a part of our daily walk with Him and that we are to spread the Good News of the gospel and the Love of Jesus through all of creation. Jesus also gives another statement to His disciples in **Matthew 9: 37-38,** which tells us, "Then he said to His disciples, 'the harvest is plentiful, but the laborers are few; therefore pray earnestly to the Lord of the harvest to send out laborers into His harvest" (ESV, 2024). Knowing just in these two verses that the harvest is plentiful and we are to go out into world to proclaim the good news is most encouraging. We see in these two verses that seeds are being planted in hearts every single day, and hearts are being softened. Jesus has set up the harvest so we can continue to build His church.

The first thing that comes to mind when thinking about evangelism is people who go to the streets and preach the gospel, then are attacked with hatred and crude remarks. Now it is true that this happens, so how do we actually apply Scripture to this, knowing that the enemy will attack at any given moment when we are waging war in his territory? This first fundamental is to know where our power needs to come from, and that is the Holy Spirit. **Acts 1:8** says, "…but you will receive power when the Holy Spirit has come upon you, and you will be my witnesses in Jerusalem and in all Judea and Samaria, and to the end of the earth" (ESV, 2024). The Holy Spirit will give us power to proclaim the good news where ever God takes us to deliver His message.

The second fundamental is to always have a mind and heart set upon Christ Jesus that will not waiver from our faith standing on the solid rock of the Word of God. In order to do this we have to maintain a clear and pure heart and sound mind that is renewed daily in the Word of God. **2 Timothy 4:5** states, "As for you, always be sober-minded, endure suffering, do the work of an evangelist, fulfill your ministry" (ESV, 2024). Having a sober mind helps us in times of discernment so that we may hear clearly the guidance and direction of the Holy Spirit. If were are to have an altered state of mind the truth of the Word of God can quickly become twisted and deceptive, making a lie from the enemy seem to be a truth.

The third fundamental to evangelism is being able to adapt to different personalities and characters so we draw them closer to God and not push them away from the Truth. **1 Corinthians 9:22** reminds us, "To the weak I became weak, that I might win the weak. I have become all things to all people, that by all means I might save some" (ESV, 2024). Here we are given a prime example of how we can adapt to the people around us without becoming worldly. We need to be in the world but not of it.

Something I learned long ago was that people don't often remember what you tell them, but they will remember how you made them feel. So being able to adapt to different personalities and maintain your integrity, your faith, your dedication to the Lord, is of most importance. People will remember this because it will make them feel different. The feeling that most people will have is a feeling of acceptance and understanding when we are able to adapt to the person in front of us. This also makes us as an evangelist listen with the intent to understand what that person is saying. Now it should be clear why being sober minded and relying on the power of the Holy Spirit are so important when evangelizing.

The fourth fundamental is knowing that we are replicating why Jesus came to earth. **John 3:16** says, "For God so loved the world, that he gave His only begotten Son, that whoever believes in Him should not perish but have eternal life." Pay close attention to the word begotten; this is a special word that in Hebrew (*Yalad*) means to be set apart, generate, birthed, bring forth, be delivered. We evangelize because Jesus came to evangelize to the lost so that they may have eternal life. That has so much Love behind it; this alone should take us to our knees to worship Our Lord and Savior.

Now there are many more fundamentals to evangelism but we are touching on the core fundamentals. Evangelizing really challenges the believer on every level, especially in the believer's acknowledgement of the Lord to other people in public. Remember what we are told in **Luke 12:8-10,** "And I tell you, everyone who confesses Me before men, the Son of Man will confess him also before the angels of God; but he who denies Me before men will be denied before the angels of God. And everyone who speaks a word against the Son of Man, it will be forgiven him; but he who blasphemes against the Holy Spirit, it will not be forgiven him."

Taking this scripture, most people who are evangelized only joke about Jesus, not knowing or understanding what blaspheming the Holy Spirit really means. To the believer, this should bring comfort in knowing that reaching the lost is hard, but it is also easy if we have our core fundamentals in practice. We are softening the hearts so God can work in the lost individual to bring them to salvation and eternal life in Him. We know this because we were once lost before we knew Jesus as our Lord and Savior. **Romans 5:8** tells us, "But God shows His own love toward us, in that while we were yet sinners, Christ died for us." Knowing we were once lost and wretched helps make it easier to adapt to the people around us so we can soften the heart and allow God's Word to penetrate the lost heart.

There are some specific things we should take into account when evangelizing to the lost. I will list a few thing below to reflect on for this lesson's discussion questions. Take some time to think about these and how they apply to your daily reading of the Word of God, your relationship with Jesus, and reaching the lost.

Answering questions with questions
Knowing when to give a direct answer from the scriptures
What to do with an intellectual argument
Converse with someone of a different religion
Being used as a vessel for God, letting God do His work

Lesson 12

Memory Verse:
Try your best to memorize the Biblical verse. It is ok to struggle with this as memorization can be difficult. Be sure to extend grace towards one another in memorizing Bible verses. This is to help create consistency and develop a good habit of thinking about Scripture throughout the day.

> ***Romans 10:17:*** *"So faith comes from hearing, and hearing through the Word of Christ."*

Quiet times:
Personal time of devotion and dedication, spending time in the Scriptures with the Lord.
Romans 10: 14 – 18 (Monday – Wednesday)
2 Corinthians 5: 20 – 21 (Thursday – Saturday)
Matthew 5: 13 – 16 (Monday – Wednesday)
Acts 2: 37 – 41 (Thursday – Saturday)

During you quiet times follow these guidelines and write them in a journal or notebook so that you will be able to share your quiet time with your group. Share at least one quiet time with your group. Before sharing a quiet time, please begin by having one of your brothers pray over the group.

Quiet Time – Guideline:

- Be specific in your answers, writing a paragraph for each answer.
- Key point or theme of the passage/verse – What is the author's intent to the original audience?
- Key Words – Repeated words in the text
- Emphasize word - Use a concordance or Bible dictionary to find what the context of the word means in your key verse.
- How will the application of the biblical principle make a difference in your daily walk with the Lord?
- Rewrite your key verse to make it personal to our modern time, without reading yourself into the text.
- How will this verse help you approach a lost person and tell them the love of Jesus?
- What is the original intent of the author to the original audience?
- Is there a biblical principle from the original audience we can apply in our modern time?
- What are the differences and similarities between the original audience and our modern audience?

Lesson 12 Discussion Questions:

Before sharing your quiet time with the group, pray that your discussion will be fruitful and encouraging to one another. Go around the group and pray over your conversation.

1. When was the last time God gave you the opportunity to evangelize or share the Good News of the gospel with a lost person?
2. Were you able to share the Good News with this lost person? Was there a spiritual attack that prevented you from sharing the Good News of the gospel?
3. Did you ask God to allow the Holy Spirit to work through you, rather than trying to evangelize on your own strength? What happens if we operate on our own strength? What happens when we allow the power of the Holy Spirit to work through us?
4. What steps and actions will you take in order to be a true witness for Jesus when evangelizing? List five steps or actions you will take and how you will follow through.
5. Have you felt the calling to evangelism in your heart? If so, has God called you to evangelize in your own city, state, church or out of state, foreign land, 10/40 window? Have you had any confirmation on this calling from the church

body or brothers surrounding you? What were the confirmations?

6. How will evangelizing in and outside the church affect the heart of a person? Why does this matter to the individual's eternal life?

7. List four more fundamentals of evangelism other than the four core fundamental that were listed above in this chapter.

8. Are you ready to quiet your mind and heart before Our Lord to hear your calling? Are you ready for guidance and direction from the Holy Spirit? Are you committed to sharing the Good News of Jesus Christ, Our Lord and Savior?

9. What is stopping you today from sharing the Good News of the gospel with the lost and the believer in the church body? What is tugging at your heart to share this Good News? If something is stopping you from sharing the Good News, will you allow your brothers to pray for you now?

10. Not everyone is called into evangelism. For those who are, will you take a stand and pray for them that they have clear and guided direction from the Holy Spirit? Will you help encourage and build up your brothers when they are down and feeling defeated?

Exercise Plan – Week 5 and Week 6

Monday
- DB side lateral raises - 5 set x 12, 10, 10, 10, 8/16, 8/16
- Barbell squat – 5 set x 12, 10, 10, 10, 8/16, 8/16
- Leg extensions – 5 set x 12, 10, 10, 10, 8/16, 8/16
- Leg curls – 5 set x 12, 10, 10, 10, 8/16, 8/16
- 20 minutes of cardio – seated row, jog, run, elliptical, bike riding, swimming

Tuesday
- Seated DB presses - 4 x 12, 12, 10, 8/16
- Seated bent over rear delt raises - 4 x 12, 12, 10/20, 10/20
- Cable side raises - 4 x 12, 12, 10, 10 Cable in front of the body or behind.
- DB front raises - 4 x 12, 12, 10, 10/10/10 Last set is a drop set. Decrease the weight each time by 5-10lbs and continue to get 10 reps until you can no longer get 10 reps.
- Shrugs with DB - 6-8 sets x Failure (use a weight that is within 80-85% of your max rep)

- 20 minutes cardio – seated row, jog, run, elliptical, bike riding, swimming

Wednesday
- Bent-over dumbbell row – 4x 12, 12, 10, 8/20
- One-arm dumbbell row – 4x 12, 12, 10, 8/20
- Wide-Grip lat pulldown – 4x 12, 12, 10, 8/20
- Standing Dumbbell triceps extension – 4x 15, 15, 12, 10/20
- 20 minutes cardio – seated row, jog, run, elliptical, bike riding, swimming

Thursday – Sunday

This time is intentionally reserved for family time. Do something active with your family like going for a walk, biking on trails, playing outdoor games in the back yard. This time should be an enjoyable fulfillment to your heart, to recognize the gift God has given you with your family.

About Kharis Publishing:

Kharis Publishing, an imprint of Kharis Media LLC, is a leading Christian and inspirational book publisher based in Aurora, Chicago metropolitan area, Illinois. Kharis' dual mission is to give voice to under-represented writers (including women and first-time authors) and equip orphans in developing countries with literacy tools. That is why, for each book sold, the publisher channels some of the proceeds into providing books and computers for orphanages in developing countries so that these kids may learn to read, dream, and grow. For a limited time, Kharis Publishing is accepting unsolicited queries for nonfiction (Christian, self-help, memoirs, business, health and wellness) from qualified leaders, professionals, pastors, and ministers. Learn more at: https://kharispublishing.com/

www.ingramcontent.com/pod-product-compliance
Lightning Source LLC
Chambersburg PA
CBHW070152100426
42743CB00013B/2885